PRODUCTIVE
PARENTING
SKILLS

Robert R. Carkhuff, Ph.D.
CARKHUFF INSTITUTE OF HUMAN TECHNOLOGY

Copyright © 1985 by
Human Resource Development Press, Inc.

22 Amherst Rd.
Amherst, Masasachusetts 01002
(413) 253-3488
1-800-822-2801

Bernice R. Carkhuff, Publisher
Elizabeth Grose, Editor

First Edition, 1985

Library of Congress Cataloging in Publication Data
International Standard Book Number 0-87425-020-X

Cover Design by Dorothy Fall
Word processing by Susan Kotzin
Composition by Magazine Group
Printing and Binding by Bookcrafters

God Made the Children

God made the children,
In all sizes and shapes,
In all kinds of colors,
And all kinds of ways.

God made the children
To make harmony,
To make sounds of life
And variety.

God noticed adults
All looked alike.
He made the children
To break up the type.

You were His children
He really loved you
Now you are adults
It's time to love true.

And so he sends down
His children to you,
To see how you treat them,
To see what you do.

God made the children
To see if you're true.
For how you treat them,
He will treat you.

R.R.C.

ABOUT THE AUTHOR

Dr. Robert R. Carkhuff is the most-referenced counseling psychologist according to Division 17, American Psychological Association. He is Chairman, Carkhuff Institute of Human Technology, a non-profit institute dedicated to the development and implementation of human resource development, training and performance programs in home, school, work and community settings.

The American Institute for Scientific Information ranks Dr. Carkhuff as the second youngest of the 100 most-cited social scientists, including such historical figures as Dewey, Freud and Marx. He is also author of three of the 100 most-referenced texts, including his two-volume classic, *Helping and Human Relations*.

Dr. Carkhuff is known as the originator of helping models and human resource development skills programs. He is also parent of the Human Technology movement which emphasizes models, systems and technologies for individual performance and organizational productivity. His most recent books on the topics of human resource development and productivity are *Sources of Human Productivity* and *The Exemplar: the Exemplary Performer in the Age of Productivity*.

PREFACE

Productive Parenting Skills is based upon the interpersonal processing skills (*IPS*) model. The evidence for the effectiveness of the *IPS* model is extensive. The findings of more than 160 studies of approximately 160,000 recipients of training have yielded overwhelmingly positive results. In 96% of the studies and on 92% of the indices, the results have been positive. What this means is that, programmatically implemented, such a program has more than a 95% chance of succeeding in achieving human goals. Conversely, the chance of failing is random. That is the goal of this book on parenting: to equip the parents with a cognitive map of parenting and the skills to get to their goals—with a 95% probability of succeeding.

May, 1985   R.R.C.
Washington, D.C.

A Chair at the Table Was Empty

Dinner was their symbol of family unity. It was the one time that they were all together as a family. It was the one special opportunity for communication, to find out what was happening with school, sports, friends, or problems; to find out about Dad's job or Mom's meeting with the teacher. Dinner reviewed the highs and lows of family life. They all sat around the dinner table and watched each other grow—or not.

They had struggled so hard to be a family. It was not easy, with all the forces undermining the family, and all the talk about kids "doing their own thing"; and now, social pressures concerning "alternatives to family living." School didn't help. It seemed so many of the ideas the kids learned at school were just the opposite of Mom's and Dad's. But in the face of these odds, Mom and Dad kept struggling. They stood together, answering the children's challenges to tradition with a united front.

Dad worked long hours, and more and more he brought his work home with him. He seemed preoccupied with the local economy's ups and downs—mainly downs. But he persisted in trying to hold the family together. He did seem to get frustrated more quickly. His temper was short. And the older the kids got, the shorter and more dictatorial his expressions became: "Where're you going now...I thought I said I didn't like those friends." At dinner, he just seemed to be increasingly tired and quiet in an angry sort of way. Gradually, the kids stopped including him in their dinner conversation.

But Mom never gave up. She kept her finger on many pulses, of which Dad's job was just one, and school was another. Mostly, she was concerned with helping the kids grow up. It had seemed easier when her goals were just "straight" and "strong." Then she could be heard forcefully saying, "Sit up straight" and "Throw your shoulders back." Anyway, Dad helped out on the "straight" and "strong" part. But now, Mom knew there had to be more. Sure, there was the "smart" part: "Study hard so that you can make something of yourself." But that wasn't quite what she needed, and she had always hoped Dad would supply the missing ingredient. But he was too tired—or unaware that something was missing. The urgency of her unfulfilled needs kept her awake nights, and yet she didn't know how to fill them. Her dinner conversation constantly searched for answers from her children, who didn't have any solutions.

Gradually, the kids slipped away. The older they got, the further away they got. Physically, they still sat at the dinner table. Only now they didn't even pretend to answer their mother's urgent pleas. It wasn't like they were declaring their autonomy to search out new directions. It was more like the old directions no longer held them. In the way a mountain climber tries to grasp a struggling partner's hand, the grip gave way, and the fingers parted. But it wasn't clear who was falling and who was left standing on the precipice—the kids, or the parents!

Mom and Dad had been so sure of themselves in the early years. And the kids had been so sure of them. The kids had wanted to achieve in response to their parents' dreams. "You're going to make your Mommy and Daddy so proud," they heard over and over in happy dinner conversation.

Somehow, in the middle years, things changed, although not abruptly! It was just that instead of concentrating on "looking good," Mom and Dad gradually seemed to shift to not "looking bad." "Whatever you do, don't make us look bad. We raised you and put a lot of effort into you. Don't let us down."

Now, in the later years, all of that is over. They don't talk about how they may look—good or bad. They don't even look at each other anymore. They just sit at dinner with heads hung, silently viewing their food.

If they did look, they would see that another chair at the dinner table was empty.

TABLE OF CONTENTS

PRETEST

Parental Age—
A Pre-Test for Parenting

In this age of human rights, everyone focuses upon his or her own needs. There are union rights and management rights; teacher rights and student rights; parent's rights and children's rights. But no one focuses upon the *right* of parenting!

Do we have a *right* to bring another human being into this world? Do we have a *right* to intervene in his or her life? Do we have a *right* to make decisions for our children? At best, these are most difficult and troubling questions.

A Question of "Right"

In order to addres this issue of *rights*, we must answer the basic question of life. Why are we here? Or, more fundamentally, what is life all about?

The only answer to this question is growth. Life is about growth. All manner of life yields to this dictum. Plants and animals alike, given the conditions of their environmental support, grow to their fullest and in so doing are completely alive. And in flowering, they live on in the growth of their progeny!

So it is with the human species. The only reason to live is to grow. This is the fundamental law of the healthy human. This is the fundamental *right* of the human child.

Life is Growth

Questions of the structure and function of growth follow. We grow physically in bone and muscle, in size and strength. We grow emotionally in perception and experience and feelings. We grow intellectually in imagery and reason, and above all, skills.

If life is growth and growth is the fundamental *right* of the human child, then we have defined the *right* of parenting and, by implication, its responsibility, necessary resources and role.

We have the *right* to be parents only when we are equipped with everything within our power to nourish the growth of our children. We are both model and agent for our children's growth—physically, emotionally and intellectually. If we have ourselves "together" and have grown to our fullest, we provide our children with a model of growth to imitate. **And imitation is the most basic source of learning**. If we have ourselves "together" and know all that we need to know to facilitate the growth of our children, we can be the agent of our children's growth.

The "Right" to Parent

Parenting, in short, is helping our children grow. This means that before we can help our children grow, we must have growing relationships with others. Before we can have growing relationships, we must be growing ourselves.

The right of parenting begins with us as individuals. It then extends to us as partners in relationships such as marriage.

We are either growing or deteriorating. There is no middle ground. Standing still is the first phase of our decline.

This is an important point which we must pause to consider. Indeed, it is the assumption upon which this entire work is based. And its implications for parenting are profound.

For if we have ceased to grow, how can we expect growth in our children? To be sure, impelled by the biological urge to grow, children will grow in their early years—emotionally and intellectually as well as physically. But in the absence of the models and agents for healthy growth, crises will catch up with them in their adolescence and young adulthood.

Helping Children Grow

The Parental Age

If we do not have ourselves "together," then we may retard, and even cause the deterioration of, our children. In my years as a practicing psychologist and educator, I have found, for example, many instances where the emotional age of the parent has been an inhibiting factor upon the growth and development of the children. This has led me to the development of what we call the *parental age* or, appropriately, "P.A." for short.

The parental age is simply an estimate of the level of parenting responsibility. In other terms, it is an index of the maturity of the parent. In Table 1, we see a checklist of parent activities or functions. If you wish to obtain an estimate of your parental age, you may do so simply by asking and answering the questions involved. Your parental age, or P.A., is the last parenting function that you have checked or affirmed, provided you have checked *all* functions below that level. You may have difficulty affirming many of the functions because of the requirement that you accomplish each function each day. The difficulty is then compounded by the number of children you have. However, we have found that the consistency of parenting performance is what pays dividends in children's growth. The frustration of busy schedules and numbers of children are no excuse for ineffective parenting. If you cannot function effectively, then expect problems in direct proportion to your non-performance.

P.A. = Parental Age

Table 1. Checklist for Estimating Parental Age

PARENTING AGE (P.A.)	CHECK	PARENTING FUNCTIONS
10	_____	Do I see that my child is properly fed, rested and clothed each day?
11	_____	Do I hold my child each day?
12	_____	Do I look carefully at my child each day?
13	_____	Do I listen attentively to what my child has to say each day?
14	_____	Do I respond to my child's behavior each day?
15	_____	Do I respond to my child's feelings each day?
16	_____	Do I help my child to understand the reason for the feeling each day?
17	_____	Do I help my child understand his or her problems each day?
18	_____	Do I help my child understand his or her goals each day?
19	_____	Do I help my child achieve his or her goals each day?
20	_____	Do I help my child develop and achieve new goals each day?
21	_____	Do I teach my child some new skill each day?

We have chosen not to illustrate any parental functions below P.A. 10 beneath which exists an infinite variety of losing strategies. There is an inexhaustible supply of parental pathology.

The basic assumption that dominates at the lower levels of functioning is this: the system, whatever its nature, was set up to serve the parent, i.e., the "world revolves around me." At one point in *child* development this may be appropriate behavior. But the family does not exist to support the parent! (No, George, just because you were here first does not mean that parenting is for the parent.) And no amount of temper tantrums will make it so. Below P.A. 10, parents can expect crises on a daily basis as they compete with their children for what neither can deliver to the other. Below P.A. 10, whatever is happening may be termed "ranting." But it is not parenting!

Parenting Versus Ranting

P.A. 10 provides us with a baseline for parenting. It simply refers to meeting the child's basic life necessities of food, rest and clothing on a regular, daily basis. If you cannot consistently check the item at P.A. 10, then you are not ready for parenting or training for the same. You must first learn how to help yourself. You may do this by finding an effective "parent" or surrogate parent who will provide a positive model. Such a person can help raise your level of functioning to the point where perhaps someday you can "get outside of your own skin" in order to care physically for another person.

"Do I see that my child is properly fed, rested and clothed each day?"

P.A. 10

P.A. 11 refers to the basic physical contact of holding or hugging your child each day. Such a response communicates love and concern for the welfare of the child. It also elicits the principle of reciprocal response, through which the child communicates concern in a similar way. Such a response at the beginning and/or end of each day communicates that, whatever else has happened, the child can depend upon the parent. With such a basic response, anything else is possible. Without it, nothing really effective is possible.

"Do I hold my child each day?"

At P.A. 12, the response indicates the degree to which the parent observes the child each day. Observation is our greatest source of learning about our children. We can observe them physically for cues to their energy and activity level. We can observe them emotionally for their level of feeling and any problems which they may be experiencing. We can observe them intellectually for indices of their mental alertness as well as their productivity and creativity. If we observe our children, then we know something about them, their strengths as well as their needs. If we do not observe them, we have only what we bring to the parenting relationship, and we will tend to impose it upon them.

"Do I look carefully
at my child each day?"

At P.A. 13, the question is, "Do I listen attentively to my child each day?" It means simply this: Do I take the time and energy to use all my senses to gather all of the input that I can from my child? Beyond infancy, the child can tell the parent most of what the parent needs to know in order to help the child grow. All it takes to discover this information is patience and discipline. Without it, you severely limit your contribution to your child's development.

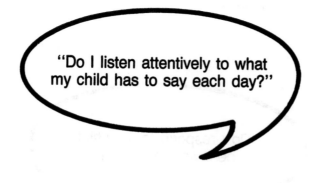

"Do I listen attentively to what my child has to say each day?"

P.A. 14 refers to the parent's response to the child's behavior. Behavior includes both verbal and nonverbal behavior. In other words, if the parent observed and, more importantly, "saw," and if the parent listened and, more importantly, "heard," then the parent must respond to the behavior. A parental response to the child's behavior gives both parent and child an opportunity to determine the accuracy of the response. Without a response, the child cannot know whether the parent has seen the behavior or heard the expression. Consequently, a parent cannot increase his or her accuracy of perception.

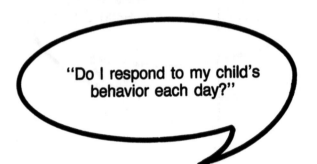

"Do I respond to my child's behavior each day?"

P.A. 15 refers to a similar response to behavior. This response tries to go beyond the behavior to understand the child's experience. The response focuses upon the child's feeling about his or her experience. Again, the function of the response is threefold: (1) to communicate an understanding about the child's experience; (2) to give the child an opportunity to check out the accuracy of the feeling response; and (3) to give the parent an opportunity to increase the accuracy of the feeling response. Without such a response, there is no way of finding out about what goes on in the child's inner world.

"Do I respond to my child's feelings each day?"

At P.A. 16, the parent is able to help the child understand the reason for his or her experience. It is not enough for the child simply to experience something. The child must also try to understand why he or she feels that way. Otherwise, the child can never do anything about the feeling. Whether the feeling is positive or negative, the child may wish to intensify or eliminate the reason for the feeling. Without understanding the reason for the feeling, the child is unable to move into new experiences or new variations of old experiences.

"Do I help my child understand the reason for the feeling each day?"

P.A. 16

Functioning at P.A. 17 the parent provides the child with an understanding of his or her problems. Problems are simply an extension of the source of negative feelings. Usually, the problems can be framed most effectively in terms of a deficit or an absence of certain skills to handle certain critical situations. Without an understanding of the problem, the child cannot work to eliminate it.

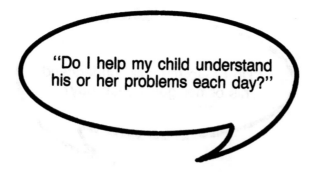

P.A. 17

$\mathbf{P}$.A. 18 refers to helping the child understand his or her goals. In other terms, the parent helps the child understand where he or she wants to go. These may be the simple goals of daily living or the very complex goals of life planning. They may come from problems the child is having or they may be initiatives on the part of the child to go somewhere that he or she has never been. Without an understanding of goals, the child is unable to formulate objectives in his or her life.

"Do I help my child understand his or her goals each day?"

At P.A. 19, the parent can help the child achieve goals. It is not enough to simply formulate goals. The parent must help the child develop step-by-step programs to achieve these goals. The more systematic the steps to the goals, the higher the probability that the child will achieve the goal. Without the development of all the steps to the goal, the child has no assurance of ever achieving his or her goal.

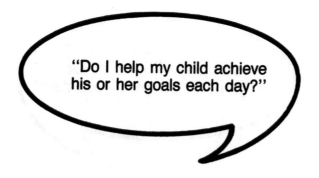

"Do I help my child achieve his or her goals each day?"

P.A. 19

At P.A. 20, the parent is able to help the child transfer his or her learning to new situations. In other words, goal achievement in one area is transferred to goals in other areas. This is a very high level of parenting which involves helping the child generalize or transfer their learning. Without this transfer of learning, the child is restricted to the learning he or she has received and unable to generalize the learning to other situations.

"Do I help my child develop and achieve new goals each day?"

P.A. 20

Parents functioning at P.A. 21 are able to teach their children to *do* all the things which they have been *helping* them do. By the time your child has become an adult, you will have successfully trained yourself out of your job. You will have equipped your child with all the skills he or she needs in order to accomplish all previous items on his or her own. This means that the child is able to care and attend, observe and listen, respond to behavior and feeling, understand reasons, problems and goals, achieve goals, develop new goals and acquire new skills on his or her own each day. In summary, the child is able to function autonomously in his or her daily living as well as life planning. Without the teaching of these skills, the child remains dependent upon the parent.

"Do I teach my child some new skill each day?"

P.A. 21

If you checked all items, including the item for P.A. 21, you are to be commended as an effective parent. You may not need this book, except possibly to consolidate your own learning. But there are obviously levels higher than P.A. 21. Remember to be honest evaluating your-self as a parent. We have found in the past that those people who tend to estimate themselves at the highest levels of functioning are often functioning at the lowest levels. Conversely, those who make more moderate estimates of themselves are more accurate in their estimates.

Calculating Your P.A.

The Parenting Formula

In our experience, we have found that effective parenting takes place when the child is two or more years younger chronologically than the P.A. of the parent. Thus, the parent can contribute to the child's growth in much the same way that an older sibling or friend can. Obviously, the greater the discrepancy in age in favor of the parent, the more effective the parenting. So that a parent functioning at P.A. 15 is more effective in parenting a chronological five-year-old than in parenting a 10- or 12-year-old.

The Parent-Child Discrepancy

In Table 2, we see an example of a parent functioning at P.A. 15. The parenting efforts are effective, it can be seen, until the child reaches 13 years of chronological age (C.A.). When the child's C.A. is within a year of the parent's P.A., parenting crises occur. The parent may, at this point, begin to retard the growth and development of the child, or threaten to do so. The parent is faced with a choice: either to grow to a higher level of parental functioning in order to retain their parenting function or to retard the growth of the child in order to continue their parental "authority."

The P.A.-C.A. Discrepancy

Table 2. The Range of Parenting Effects As a
Function of the Parental Age

		CHILD'S CHRONO-
PARENTAL AGE (P.A.)		**LOGICAL AGE (C.A.)**
	DETERIORATION OR REJECTION RANGE	⎧ 21 ⎨ 20 ⎬ 19 ⎩ 18
	RETARDATION RANGE	⎰ 17 ⎱ 16
15	CRISIS RANGE	⎰ 15 ⎱ 14
	EFFECTIVE PARENTING RANGE	13 12 11 10 9 8 7 6 5 4 3 2 1

When the child's C.A. is a year or two above the P.A., we have found that the parent begins to actively retard the child. The parent has opted for retarding the child rather than facilitating growth. This is the usual choice in spite of the potentially disasterous consequences for both parent and child. Indeed, the parents may have made this choice many years before when they themselves stopped growing. Perhaps they did so either because there were no people—biological parents or otherwise—to parent "them" or because they did not learn or could not stand the discipline of growth. Perhaps many years of conditioning solidified that choice. Or the parent may have regressed to a more comfortable, even earlier, level of functioning due to the life crises that he or she was not able to handle in an adult manner. The P.A. may in reality have deteriorated over time.

Parental Retarding

Finally, when the child is two or more years above the P.A., we have found one or two things happening. Either the child succumbs and becomes, in effect, the parent's victim and merges by a complete identification with the deterioration pattern of the parent. Possibly the child is able to reject the parent's behavior, at least that part of it which might cause his or her deterioration. This is, to be sure, the most difficult course. And it is not necessarily an effective one. For the child must find other models and agents functioning at higher P.A.'s to do the parenting for them. Attempting to parent oneself usually condemns the child to living a life in reaction to, rather than free of, the parent's behavior. And this means that the child will be limited, and will ultimately deteriorate in his or her own level of functioning. Such children will not grow into the effective parents needed to rear another generation of children, anymore than their own parents did.

Succumbing or Rejecting

If you have estimated your P.A., you may now insert it in the parenting formula illustrated in Table 3. This will predict when crises may start to occur. You may subtract two years from your estimated P.A. in order to obtain your range of parenting effectiveness. When your child's C.A. falls within a year of your P.A., you may expect crises. When your child's C.A. goes a year or two beyond your P.A., you may assume that you have already begun to retard his or her functioning in some important ways. Finally, where your child's C.A. goes two or more years beyond your P.A., you may assume that you are contributing to his or her deterioration, whether or not they are living in reaction to or identifying with you.

If your P.A. is significantly higher than your child's C.A., you may not wish to pursue this material further. Or you may just wait for the time when he or she approaches your P.A. Hopefully, you will wish to prepare yourself for this most difficult of all human responsibilities, the perpetuation of human effectiveness.

P.A.-C.A. Relationship

Table 3. Formula for Estimating Parenting Crises

MY CURRENT ESTIMATED PARENTING AGE (P.A.)		CHILD'S CHRONO- LOGICAL AGE (C.A.)
	Deterioration or Rejection Range	− Parent's P.A. + 2 or more.
	Retardation Range	− Parent's P.A. + 1 or 2
_____ P.A.	Crisis Range	− Parent's P.A. − 1
	Parenting Range	− Parent's P.A. − 2 or more

The right of parenting, then, is defined by the parent functioning at P.A. levels higher than the child's C.A. This means that, at a minimum, the parent's P.A. is at least two years higher than the child's C.A. If it is not, then there is no *right* to parent. Period! End of report—unless you choose growth for yourself and, thus, for your child.

For the right to parent is predicated upon the ability to nourish growth. And the ability to nourish growth in our children is contingent upon our ability to grow ourselves.

Like the marital union out of which it is born, parenting may be "for better or for worse."

It all depends upon the skills we have to grow to our fullest and to help our children grow to their fullest.

Whether the dinner table and our family life is full—in numbers and in people—or whether "a chair at the table is empty," depends in a very real sense upon our parental maturity and the skills we have to implement that maturity.

Parenting Skills—For Better or Worse!

I. INTRODUCTION

1. The Art of Parenting

Parenting may be the most beautiful or ugly, fulfilling or draining, rewarding or punishing human experience. It is the process by which children grow into mature adults. How much the children grow depends upon how much we, as parents, grow. If we do not know what we are doing, we will feel helpless and immobilized. Our parenting experience will be ugly, draining and punishing. If we know what we are doing, we will be confident and purposeful. Our parenting experience will be beautiful, fulfilling and rewarding.

Parenting is Helping People Grow

During crises, parenting may yield all of these experiences at once: the beautiful and the ugly; the fulfilling and the draining; the rewarding and the punishing.
But crises are only opportunities to grow—for us and
our children! So when we deal with the insolent resis-
tance at home, or the regressive rebellion at school, or
the debilitating peer-influence in the community, or the
poor work attitude on the job, we must remember that
these crises are opportunities for us to reach toward
our next level of development. Somehow we must rise
above our conditioned responses and help our children
rise above their reflex responses. How well we grow
together or how much we fall apart depends upon our
parenting skills.

Crises are Opportunities to Grow

Think for a moment of the traditional roles of mothering and fathering. Write down the three key words that define each role's traditional contributions for you. Then circle the key word and write a definition using that word. If your spouse or other people are involved, try to write a definition that includes all of the key words.

MOTHER: Key words: _____
_____
_____

Definition: A mother is _____
_____
_____
_____

FATHER: Key words: _____
_____
_____

Definition: A father is _____
_____
_____
_____

Mothering and Fathering Make Contributions

Now think for a moment about the role of parent.
Write down the three key words that define the parent's
contribution for you. Then circle the key word and write
a definition using that word. Again, if your spouse or
others are involved, try to write a definition that includes
all of the key words.

PARENT: Key words: _____

            _____

            _____

            _____

Definition: A parent is _____

            _____

            _____

            _____

Parenting Makes Contributions

In defining mothering and fathering, you may have found that you used familiar words in each of these definitions. Mother may be warm and sensitive, attentive and nourishing, caring and loving. Father may be strong and purposeful, demanding and conditional, confident and competent. To be sure, their descriptions put them at opposite ends of a continuum. These are the traditional ways that we usually conceive of the contributions of mother and father. These are the traditional roles which we are conditioned to perform as men and women. When we are functioning most effectively in either of these roles, we feel may like we are in a "groove," or that we are walking in the footsteps of our ancestors and our societies.

Mother _____ **Father**

Mothering and Fathering are Traditional Roles

In defining parenting, you may have found that you used words similar to those in your definitions of mother and father. Parents must *both* be warm and strong, nourishing and demanding, loving and competent. Indeed, in many of our parenting experiences, we find we must be both—mother in one moment, then father in the next—sometimes both simultaneously. The parent is both mother and father.

Mothering ＿＿＿＿＿＿＿＿＿ˌ＿＿＿＿＿＿＿ Fathering

The Parent is Mother and Father

However, the parent is more than the sum total of the stereotyped roles of mother and father. Moreover, parenting is a function rather than simply a sum-total of these roles. This is an especially important point today, with both mother and father often working or sharing parenting. It is also critical in the single parent family. The function of parenting is to transform children into mature adults. Immaturity means simply that the children lack the responses to function effectively in their worlds. Maturity means that they have these responses. In order to transform immature people into mature people, parents must not only be mature, they must also have parenting skills. Productive parenting skills can place the parent well above a composite definition of mother and father.

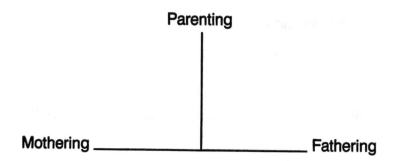

Parenting

Mothering _____ Fathering

The Parent is More Than Mother and Father

The most basic initial skill of parenting is responding. In her most effective role, the mother has been socialized to respond to the experience of her children: warmly and sensitively; attentively and nurturingly; caringly and lovingly. She enters their frames of reference because she knows intuitively the parenting principle that *child development begins with the child's frame of reference.* The mother's effectiveness in her responding role depends upon how accurately she enters her children's frames of reference. She attempts to respond accurately to capture and communicate her children's frames of reference so that they can explore where they are *in their worlds.*

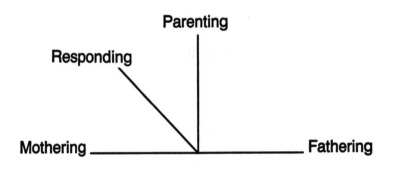

Parenting

Responding

Mothering _____ Fathering

Parents are Responders

The most basic culminating skill of parenting is initiating. In his most effective role, the father has been socialized to initiate from his experience of the world: strongly and purposefully; demandingly and conditionally; confidently and competently. He initiates from his own experience because he knows intuitively the parenting principle that *children will imitate the behavior of striving to achieve.* The father's effectiveness in his initiating role depends upon how systematically he initiates from his frame of reference. He attempts to initiate effectively to conceptualize and operationalize goals that will enable his children to *act to get to where they need to be in their worlds.*

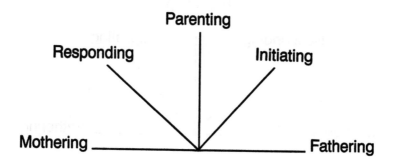

Parents are Initiators

The most basic transitional skill of parenting is personalizing or individualizing goals. Personalizing is the skill that enables the parents to not only incorporate but to use the above composite descriptions of mothering and fathering. Personalizing motivates the children by developing goals that are useful for the children from their own perspective. It is based upon the parenting principle that *growth must be instrumental for the children's purposes.* Thus, transitionally, the effective parent personalizes accurately the children's experience in order to help them to *understand where they are in relation to where they want to be in their worlds.*

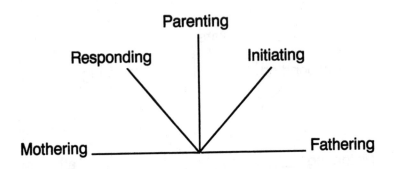

Effective Parents are Personalizers

Clearly, not all biological or surrogate parents are effective (i.e., responsive, personalizing and initiating). Indeed, the traditional feminine stereotype by which girls can be conditioned finds them in a quadrant centering around the role of mother. The feminine roles range from responding (most constructive roles) to being noniniative or passive (least constructive roles). Similarly, the traditional masculine stereotype may find boys conditioned to the quadrant centering around the role of father. These masculine roles range from initiating (most constructive roles) to nonresponsiveness or insensitivity (least constructive roles).

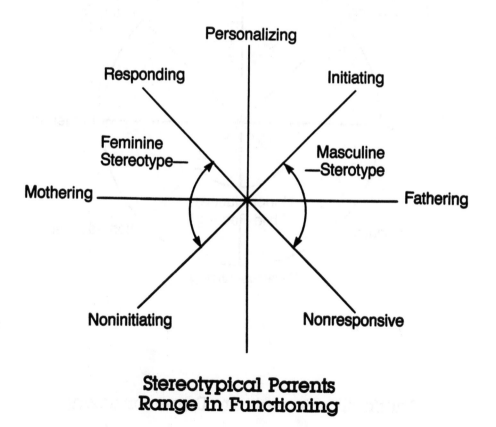

**Stereotypical Parents
Range in Functioning**

Indeed, parents without either commitment or skills can be destructive. Rather than accurately responsive, they are passively noninitiative. Rather than systematically initiative, they are insensitively nonresponsive. Rather than intensely personalizing, non-productive parents are indifferently depersonalizing. Because they are nonresponsive, depersonalizing and noninitiative, they demonstrate a negative role model for human growth and development for their children.

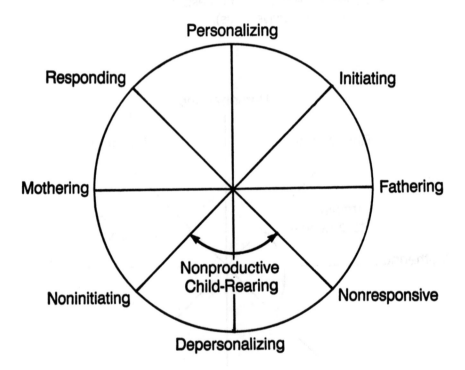

Ineffective Parents are Depersonalizing

In summary, productive parenting incorporates the most constructive roles of the responsive stereotype of mothering and the initiative stereotype of fathering while making its unique contribution of personalizing. Initially, the productive parent responds sensitively to the children's experience in order to help them explore where they are in their worlds. Transitionally, the productive parent personalizes accurately the children's experience in order to help them understand where they are in relation to where they want. Finally, the productive parent initiates systematically from his or her experience to help the children act to get from where they are to where they want to be. In short, productive parenting involves helping children explore, understand and act effectively upon their worlds. Productive parenting involves growing people.

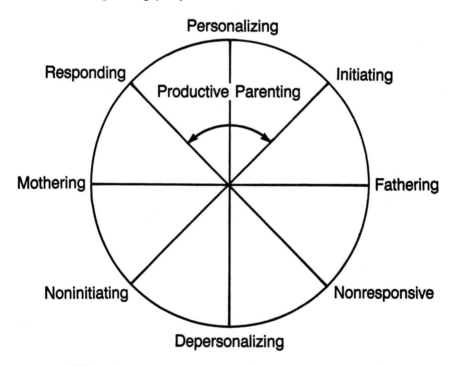

Effective Parenting Requires Growth

II. MODELS FOR PARENTING

2. The Goals of Parenting

Parenting is the most stimulating, most demanding, most rewarding job we can have. It calls for the wisdom of Solomon, the sensitivity of Ruth, the strength of Abraham and the endurance of Hannah. In our very short lifetimes, we find ourselves excited by its possibilities, agitated by its crises and panicked by its outcomes. It is all that we are and all that we can be. The goals of parenting are to help our children to become all that they are and all that they can be.

The Goal of Parenting is to Actualize the Child's Resources

Think for a moment of a child. Write down one or more key words that you would use to describe the level of the child's physical, emotional and intellectual resource development. If other resource dimensions have special meaning to you, you may also describe them.

Physical resources: _____

_____

_____

Emotional resources: _____

_____

_____

Intellectual resources: _____

_____

_____

Other resources: _____

_____

_____

Describing Immaturity

You may have found that the child's descriptions are very familiar to you. Physically, the child is small, and not ready for the demands of adult life. Emotionally, the child is dependent, unstable and egocentric—or focused around the self—as well as dependent upon others. Intellectually, the child is illiterate and irrational or incapable of solving problems and achieving goals. Also, if you have chosen to do so, you may have described the child's level of development on other dimensions. For example, socially or spiritually, the child is amoral or without moral convictions and is oriented toward consuming.

CHILD'S LEVEL OF RESOURCE DEVELOPMENT

Physical: Small and unprepared

Emotional: Unstable and egocentric

Intellectual: Illiterate and irrational

You have just defined immaturity. Immaturity is a deficit of responses that leaves the person ill-equipped to function effectively in adult life.

Immaturity is a Response Deficit

Now think for a moment about the adult. Write down one or more key words that you would use to describe the level of the adult's physical, emotional and intellectual resource development. If other resource dimensions have special meaning to you, you may also describe them.

Physical resources: _____

_____

_____

Emotional resources: _____

_____

_____

Intellectual resources: _____

_____

_____

Other resources: _____

_____

_____

Describing Maturity

The descriptions of adults are also familiar to you. Physically, the adult is full-grown and fit for the demands of life. Emotionally, the adult is stable and sociocentric or revolving around relations with others. Intellectually, the adult is literate and rational, capable of figuring out and achieving goals. You may have described the adult's development in other terms: spiritually or socially, as moral and productive; in terms of a career, as planned and independent. As can be seen, you have just defined maturity as an asset of responses that equip the person to function effectively in life.

ADULT'S LEVEL OF RESOURCE DEVELOPMENT

Physical: Full-grown and fit

Emotional: Stable and sociocentric

Intellectual: Literate and rational

Maturity is a Response Asset

Parenting is simply the slow process of transforming deficits into assets, immaturity into maturity. Thus, the goal of parenting is resource development. The physical goals for the child are to become large and fit for adult life. The emotional goals for the child are to become stable and involved with others. The intellectual goals for the child are to become literate and rational. The goal of parenting is to help the child develop his or her physical, emotional and intellectual resources.

LEVELS OF RESOURCE DEVELOPMENT

	Child	Adult
Physical:	Small and unprepared	Full-grown and fit
Emotional:	Unstable and egocentric	Stable and sociocentric
Intellectual:	Illiterate and irrational	Literate and rational

Parenting is the Process of Transforming Children Into Mature People

The goal of parenting, then, is the development of resources—physical, emotional and intellectual. The outcome by which we judge ourselves as parents, therefore, is the development of these resources. If they are well developed in our children, then we have succeeded as parents. If they are poorly developed in our ohildren, then we have failed as parents. When we choose for ourselves to be more or less than we are or can be, we choose for our children to be more or less than they are or can be.

**Effective Parenting is
Developing Resources**

3. The Process of Parenting

Parenting is one of the most important things we will ever do. And yet it is the thing for which we are least trained. Most of us simply stumble into parenthood. Maybe we were not prepared for choosing our husbands or wives. We are even less prepared for that miraculous accident of birth. It is this miracle of birth which causes us to focus upon the developmental process by which we might facilitate our children's actualization of their resources. By focusing upon the developmental process, we can find out how to help our children grow into mature adults.

The Process of Parenting is Developmental

The models for development are present in infancy. Think for a moment about how children learn in their natural state. Write some key words to characterize the sequence of learning that you have observed.

1. _____

_____

_____

2. _____

_____

_____

3. _____

_____

_____

4. _____

_____

_____

5. _____

_____

_____

Describing Naturalistic Learning

You may have found that the first year of human development serves as a prototype for all human learning. The newborn infant enters the world with few responses other than physiological reflexes. Thus, for example, the child has the sucking reflex and the palmar or grasping reflex. If the parents are responsive to the child, these reflexes will become instrumental to the child's survival. They constitute the child's initial resources in approaching a world which will lead, hopefully, to his or her developmental growth.

Reflexes

The Child Brings Reflex Responses

One of the ways in which we guide our children is by helping them form habits. Basically, human habits are behaviors that are acquired without human intelligence or learning. They may be acquired by associating or relating in space and time two or more sets of activities. At least one of these activities must satisfy some human need in order for the human behavior to be repeated as a habit. For example, the child may develop the sucking habit when nourished by the mother's breast. The results may be said to be instrumental in satisfying the child's need for nourishment. In the process, the child may develop a "conditioned" sucking response to the stimulus of the mother's nipple. In a similar manner, the child later on may develop a conditioned grasping response to the stimulus of food, which is instrumental in satisfying the child's need for nourishment. There are many other kinds of life habits which may be developed without human intelligence or intentions.

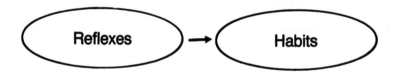

The Child Develops Habits

Human learning and, indeed, human intelligence begin to manifest themselves when the child is several months old. At this point, the children begin to explore themselves and their environments. They discover the existence and the relationship of the environment stimulus and their own responses. In other terms, children become aware of the association of the stimuli and the responses that have been conditioned to the stimuli. They become aware of causes and effects in their worlds. This awareness is reciprocal. For example, the child becomes aware that the nipple or the food serve as stimuli to a sucking or grasping response. This response, in turn, will lead to satisfying a need for nourishment. The child may also become aware that a need for nourishment stimulates the response of searching for the nipple or the food.

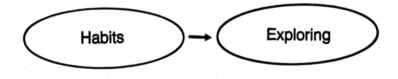

The Child Learns to Explore

It is a short step from becoming aware of the ingredients of human experience to anticipating experiences. With the increasing confidence in this awareness of the relationship of stimulus and response, the child is prepared for purposeful learning at about one year of age. In other words, the child sets out to obtain a certain end result, independent of the means. For example, the child may set out to attract mother or obtain food or an object that is out of reach. Drawing from this understanding of the relationship of stimulus and response or cause and effect, the child sets goals of achieving certain effects. The goals of the purposeful act are often only seen later, although some approximation of these goals obviously was intended from the beginning.

Exploring ➝ Understanding

The Child Learns to Understand

Finally, the child develops behavior patterns that are instrumental to achieving goals. From the end of the first year on, the child draws from his or her repertoire of behaviors to produce the response needed to achieve the goal. For example, the child may laugh or cry to get attention from one or more parents. The child may move his or her hand in the direction of the unreachable food or object. There may be a series of trial and error experiences. These experiences may confirm the child's responses through reaching the goal and experiencing satisfaction or deny the child's response through not reaching the goal.

Exploring ⟶ Understanding ⟶ Acting

The Child Learns to Act

The first year of human development serves as a prototype for all human learning. The child's reflexes are unknowingly conditioned as habitual responses to certain stimuli. Initially, the child explores and identifies the nature of the stimuli and responses in his or her experience. In the transition stage, the child comes to understand the interactive nature of stimuli and responses, anticipating the effects of one upon the other and develops goals to achieve these effects. Finally, the child acts by drawing from his or her developing repertoire of responses to attempt to achieve the goals. The child's behavior is shaped by the feedback or the effects it achieves in the environment. This feedback recycles the steps or phases of learning as the child explores more extensively, understands more accurately and acts more effectively.

Exploring ⟶ Understanding ⟶ Acting

Learning is the Source of Growth

The exact same ascending, enlarging spiral of exploration, understanding and action is the source of the maturing persons' improving repertoire of responses. In short, this developmental learning process is the source of developing human resources—the goal of parenting. Maturing persons explore where they are in relation to their worlds; understand where they want to be; and act to get there. They recycle this learning process continuously with new input and the feedback which they receive from their acting. What goes on in the first year of life goes on in more and more refined ways throughout life. How effectively we live our lives depends totally upon how efficiently and effectively we learn. How effectively our children develop their resources depends totally upon how efficiently and effectively we learn and implement our parenting skills to facilitate their learning.

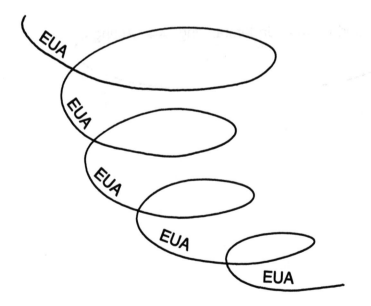

Effective Parenting Facilitates Learning

III. THE SKILLS OF PARENTING

4. Parents as Attenders

Parenting is a role for which we are unprepared. And still, the taking on of this role begins with our hopes, and even our fantasies, for our loved ones. The early moments of parenting can be like the early moments of marriage: dreams of togetherness and success; dreams of fulfillment. Spontaneously, we race each other in the middle of the night for the privilege of picking up our first born. Vigilantly, we observe their behaviors for signs of strength. Eagerly, we listen to their first utterances for signs of intelligence. Indeed, this is the time when we feel the most competent as parents.

ATTENDING

Parents are Attenders

Let us take a moment to get an index of how well we attend and observe our children. Let us take several incidents and indicate the inferences that we would make from certain appearances or behaviors of our children:

Your child lays around all day on the floor watching any and every television program.

Inference: _____

_____

_____

_____

Your adolescent sits attentively at the table reading from a stack of books and writing out a homework assignment.

Inference: _____

_____

_____

_____

Your young adult comes home calmly, looks natural and greets you casually with a "Hi."

Inference: _____

_____

_____

_____

Making Inferences from Behavior

These observances are actually very familiar and simple parenting skills. They are called attending skills. They emphasize paying attention to the obvious. This means attending physically to our children. We *attend physically* to them so that we can observe them carefully. We can learn most of what we need to know about people by *observing* them. Finally, we attend to our children so that we can *listen* to them and, most important, "hear" what they are really saying. These attending skills—attending physically, observing and listening—are necessary for involving our children as well as ourselves in a growth experience.

PARENTING SKILLS

Parent: ATTENDING

↓

Child: INVOLVING

Attending Facilitates Involvement

You may feel comfortable in making these inferences. We tend to make them sometimes, whether we know it or not. Especially, when our children come in late or following a critical situation of some kind or another!

Thus, we may infer that the child laying around watching television all day is not alert to other things going on around him or her, is not feeling particularly good—at best neutral, is not ready to become engaged in any other activity.

The adolescent child doing her homework leads us to infer that she is fully involved in her activities, is upbeat in her attitude, and is ready for learning.

The young adult appears neither strongly positive or negative. Thus, we may infer that he or she is moderate in energy, attitude and readiness for engagement.

Inferring

We can attend at high, moderate and low levels. At high levels of attending, we facilitate high levels of involvement. At moderate levels of attending, we elicit moderate levels of involvement. At low levels of attending, we elicit low levels of involvement. Indeed, the principle of reciprocal attending applies: our children usually attend to us to the same degree that we attend to them.

High   **Moderate**   **Low**

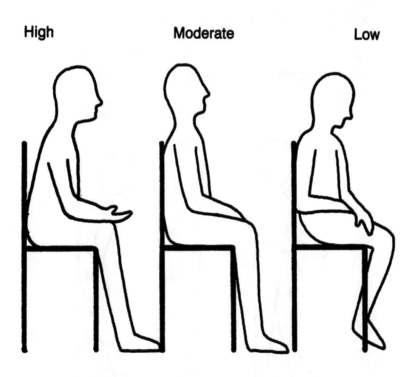

Attending Facilitates Involvement

The prototype for attending physically is the parent holding the infant child. We are in close proximity to one another. We are facing them. We are leaning toward them. Above all, we are making contact with them. These are the exact same skills that we must use to attend physically to all people.

Proximity: As close as possible—usually a few feet away

Facing: Squared—left shoulder to right shoulder, etc.

Leaning: 20° sitting and 10° standing

Eyeing: Making eye contact

When we use these skills, we not only communicate our attentiveness, but we also prepare ourselves for observing.

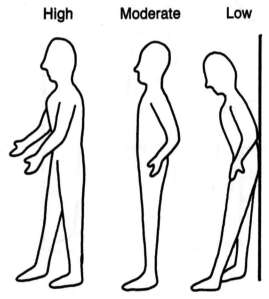

High   Moderate   Low

Attending Physically Focuses Attention

When we attend physically, we can observe accurately. When we observe, we notice the appearance and behavior of our children. Their appearance tells us how they prepared for that moment—where they were or what they were doing prior to that moment. This behavior tells us where they are in the moment. When we focus upon appearance, we can observe the quality of their personal hygiene, clothes and hair and the condition of their bodies, skin and eyes. When we focus upon behavior, we can observe the exact same qualities that comprise attending physically. Are they involved in high, moderate or low levels of attending in the moment? Are they squaring, leaning and making eye contact with us, or with whatever they are engaged in?

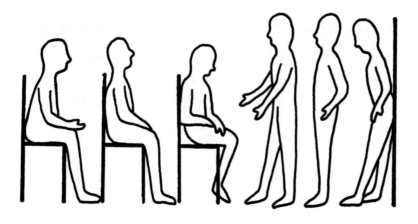

Observing Focuses Upon Behavior

Our children's level of attentiveness is the richest source of our learning about them in the moment. We can make physical, emotional and intellectual inferences from their attending behavior. If they are engaged in a high level of attending, then we may infer that they are physically alert and full of energy, emotionally "up" and intellectually ready for whatever task is at hand. If they evidence a low level of attending, then we may infer that they are physically drained, emotionally "down" and intellectually unready for the task at hand. If there are no clear behavioral indications, we may make neutral inferences. However, we must be vigilant in continuing to observe our children's behavior because they are either moving toward growth or deteriorating at any given point in time.

INFERENCES FROM LEVELS OF ATTENTIVENESS

Levels of Attentiveness	Physical	Emotional	Intellectual
High	Alert	Up	Ready
Moderate	Neutral	Neutral	Neutral
Low	Drained	Down	Not Ready

Observing Facilitates Making Inferences

Equipped with our inferences from observation, we are now ready to listen to our children's verbal expressions of their experience. In order to listen effectively to our children, we must do at least four things. We must suspend our own personal judgements, at least initially. We must know what we are listening for (i.e., the cues to our children's physical energy, emotional feelings and intellectual acuity). We must resist distractions, positioning ourselves to avoid noises, a compelling view, other people—anything that will take away our attention from our children. Finally, we must make a verbatim recall of our children's expressions to ourselves. We can rate our accuracy of recall. Remember, most of us have been conditioned not to "hear." We tend to be apprehensive about the implications of this type of intimacy. So we must work very hard to listen actively and to recall.

High accuracy   — Verbatim recall of expression

Moderate accuracy — Recall of gist of expression

Low accuracy   — Little or no recall of expression

Listening Focuses Upon Expressions

Productive parenting, then, emphasizes the same attending skills that we used when our children were infants. We must practice these skills and learn to use them throughout our children's development and become as comfortable with our children as we were when they were infants. Again, the function of attending is to give our children the feelings of security that make their growing possible. When they have begun to express personally relevant experiences, they have signaled their readiness for us to respond and communicate our understanding. Attending skills are the necessary but not sufficient conditions of parenting. With them, productive parenting, *and* all of our hopes and dreams are possible. Without them, productive parenting is not possible.

**Productive Parenting
Emphasizes Attending**

5. Parents as Responders

From the moment of our birth, life has been a head-long plunge into a confusing, often overwhelming array of human experiences. The warm and tender moments when we get outside of ourselves to respond to another person is reward in itself. We feel "full" even in the absence of each other.

But we do not always know how to create or sustain these moments. The cold and tedious hours when we are trapped by our own need for safety dominate our sense of self. And then we feel alone even in the presence of each other, and unable to repond.

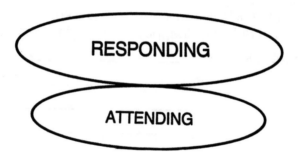

Parents are Responders

Let us take a moment to get an index of how well we respond to our children. Let us take several incidents and try to formulate the most helpful responses that we might make to our children.

Your child has just finished a drawing and rushes to you and exclaims:

"Mommy! Daddy! Look what I did!"

Parent response: _____

_____

_____

_____

Your teenager (11-12), who has just been cut from one of the activities which he or she tried out for, comes in radiating disappointment, saying nothing.

Parent response: _____

_____

_____

_____

Your teenager who has been increasingly verbal in asserting independence blurts out his or her rejection of the rules:

"There's no way I'm coming home by 11 o'clock."

Parent response: _____

_____

_____

_____

Formulating Responses

You may have found yourself feeling frustrated because it was so difficult to formulate a response. And yet these are responding skills we must learn in order to be skilled parents. Let us check ourselves out.

You might have responded to the child's feelings of happiness or excitement or pride expressed for the meaningful activity of drawing:

"You feel so happy with yourself because it is such a good drawing."

You might have responded to the teenager's feelings of sadness or hopelessness about the meaningful experience of not making the squad:

"You're feeling sad because it meant so much to you."

You might have responded to the teenager's feelings of anger and hostility in relation to his or her meaningful search for independence:

"You feel angry with me because I put controls on you."

Responding to Children

Ÿou may feel concerned because you did respond as you would like to. You can easily learn to respond effectively as a parent by learning responding skills. The responding skills emphasize the content of the child's expression; the feeling underlying the child's expression; and the meaning of or the reason for the feeling. Together, these responding skills enable us to facilitate our children's explorations of where they are in relation to their experiences of their worlds and the significant people in their worlds.

PARENTING SKILLS

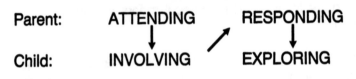

Responding to Human Experience

After we have learned to respond verbatim to our children's expressions, we must learn to communicate our understanding of the content of these expressions. If the expressions are short and to the point, we can use the exact words of our children. If the expressions are longer and more rambling, we can paraphrase the expression or attempt to capture the essence of the expression. We can use the reflective format, "You're saying _____," in communicating our understanding of the content of their expressions. Thus, for example, we can capture the content of the child's expression: "You're saying that you made the team," or "You're saying that you got cut from the team." We respond to content to insure our accuracy in understanding and to lay a base for responding to feeling.

"You're saying _____."

Responding to Content

When we have laid a base of responses to content, we can then attempt to respond to feeling. We can simply stop and reflect upon our responses to content as if we were our children. We can ask ourselves, given those experiences, "How would it make me feel?" We can identify "feeling words" which capture the feeling of the experience. Thus, if the child made the team, he or she, for example, might feel happy. Or, if the child got cut from the team, he or she might feel sad. We can use the reflective format, "You feel _____," to communicate our understanding of the feeling of the experience. Thus, "You feel happy" or "You feel sad" might be accurate responses to feeling.

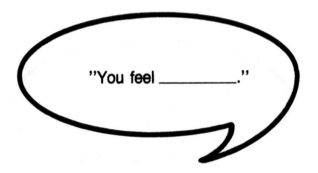

"You feel _____."

Responding to Feeling

Every feeling has a reason. We must also communicate our understanding of the meaning of the experience or the reason for the feeling. To capture the meaning, we must simply use the content to provide the reason for the feeling. Thus, for example, the child can be happy because he or she made the team or sad because he or she got cut from the team. We can use the responding format, "You feel _____ because _____," to capture the feeling and the meaning of the experience. Thus, "You feel happy because you made the team" or "You feel sad because you got cut from the team" might be accurate responses to the child's experience.

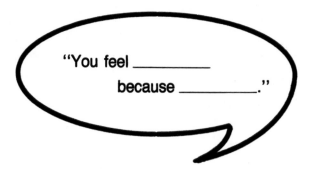

"You feel _____ because _____."

Responding to Feeling and Meaning

Productive parenting, then, emphasizes responding skills that enable us to enter another person's frame of reference and to communicate our understanding of that frame of reference. The function of responding is to give our children the message that we are understanding, accurately, what they are communicating to us. We are accepting them and communicating our understanding of their experiences at the level they are expressing them. In effect, we are attempting to communicate interchangeably with their expressions of their experience. When they are ready to personalize their problems and goals, they will signal their readiness for us to go beyond what they are saying. Our responding skills allow us to "get outside of our skins" and incorporate our children's experience into our own.

Productive Parenting Emphasizes Responding Sensitively

6. Parents as Personalizers

While it begins with our hopes, parenting is plagued by our fears. It is interrupted with increasing frequency by our anxieties about failing. Later, we are almost relieved when our anxieties are transformed into fears and we can focus upon our failures. In the absence of direction, failures often give us specifics we can do something about. And yet we were so sure of ourselves as parents when we were young. And our children were so sure of us. As time goes on, we may have lost confidence in each other. Reluctantly, we view the "report cards" of life. Blindly, we pick our way through increasingly difficult decisions which require finer and finer discriminations. Sometimes we make the wrong decisions, because no one ever taught us how to make the right ones. If it is this way for us, how can it be more for our children?

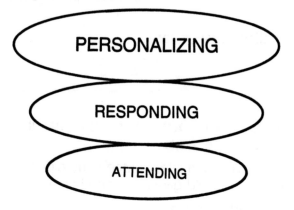

Parents are Personalizers

Let us take a moment to get an index of how well we personalize our children's experience. Let us take several incidents with our children and try to personalize or individualize their experiences by determining the real problems and goals implied by the expression:

Your child comes running in, crying and apparently feeling hurt, saying:

"He never lets me play with him."

Personalized response: _____

_____

_____

_____

_____

Your teenager has just reluctantly showed you his report card for your signature, saying:

"Old Mr. Baker—he just doesn't like me. Whatever I do is not good enough for him. He's just against me."

Personalized response: _____

_____

_____

_____

_____

Your teenager, after getting home later than the agreed upon time, adds:

"I'm sorry that I'm late, but the party didn't start 'til late so no one could give me a ride home until now."

Personalized response: _____

_____

_____

_____

_____

Formulating Personalized Responses

You may have found these personalized responses quite difficult to make. And yet these are precisely the crises that are turning points of parenting.

You might have personalized the problem and the missed goal the child was implying by her expression of hurt:

"You feel sad because you can't play with him and you really want to."

You might have personalized the problem and goal that the teenager was implying by her expression of anger:

"You feel disappointed with yourself because you can't seem to get Mr. Baker on your side, although you'd like very much to do so."

You might have personalized the problem and goal that the teenager was implying by his expression of sorrow:

"You feel apologetic because you couldn't get your act together and you really want to."

Personalizing Responses with our Children

You may feel disappointed in yourself because you can't personalize your children's experiences. You can easily learn to respond effectively as a parent by learning personalizing skills. Personalizing skills emphasize internalizing responsibility for the experience; personalizing the response deficit problems and, thus, the response asset goals; and personalizing the changed feeling. Together, these personalizing skills enable us to facilitate our children's understanding of their real constructive goals in their worlds.

PARENTING SKILLS

Parent: ATTENDING RESPONDING PERSONALIZING

Child: INVOLVING EXPLORING UNDERSTANDING

Personalizing Human Experience

Personalizing meaning is outlining the personal implications of the experience for the child, i.e., the child feels a certain way because of what *he* or *she* did or did not do rather than what *someone else* did or did not do. It is the difference between internalizing responsibility and externalizing responsibility for an experience. For the parents this means that instead of saying, "You feel _____ because _____," we may use the personalizing meaning format, "You feel _____ because you _____." For example, while a parent may have responded to a child who feels the teacher is picking on him or her, "You feel hurt because he is always picking on you;" the parent can personalize the meaning by internalizing the responsibility for the experience: "You feel hurt because you are always being picked on by him."

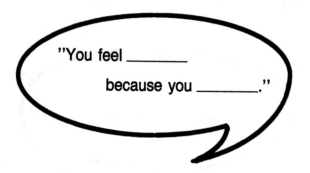

Personalizing Meaning

It is a short but important step from personalizing the meaning to personalizing the problem. When we consider the personal implications for the child, we must also consider the child's personal problems which contributed to creating the experience. Foremost among these problems is the lack of responses the child has for handling the situation. The initial thrust of all parenting is being able to define the response deficit of the child. The parent may use the personalizing problem format, "You feel _____ because you cannot _____." Thus, in responding to the child who is being picked on, the parent may personalize the problem. "You feel hurt because you cannot relate to the teacher, and he always ends up picking on you." In this manner, we facilitate the child's understanding of his or her responsibility in creating the experience. Personalizing the problem enables the child to internalize the responsibility for the response deficit.

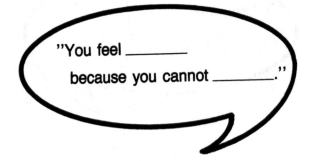

"You feel _____ because you cannot _____."

Personalizing Problems

The second thrust of all parenting is to facilitate the transformation response deficits into assets. When the child internalizes the responsibility for the response deficit, he or she is inspired to change the deficits into assets. It is a simple step to respond to the child in terms of the goals implied by the personalized problems. The parent may use the personalizing goal format, "You feel _____ because you cannot _____ and you really want to _____." Thus, in response to the "picked-upon" child, the parent may personalize the goal, "You feel hurt because you cannot relate to the teacher, and you would really like to get along with him." In this manner, we transform the child's personalized problem into an individualized goal. Personalizing the goal helps to define the constructive outcome emerging from all problem presentations.

"You feel _____ because you cannot _____ and you really want to _____."

Personalizing Goals

Finally, since we have personalized the problem and goal, we must now personalize the feeling. All parenting should respond to the disappointment which the children experience when they understand the personalized problem, i.e., that they lack the responses which they need to handle a situation effectively. All parenting should also respond to the children's motivation when they understand the personalized goal. The parents may use a format similar to that which they used for personalizing the goal, "You feel _____ because you cannot _____ and you're really _____." Thus, for the "picked-upon" child, the parent may personalize the new feelings: "You feel disappointed because you cannot relate to the teacher, and you're really eager to try to learn how." In this manner, we individualize the child's internalized feelings. Personalizing the feelings completes the personalizing process, provided we stay constantly focused upon the subtle resources in feelings.

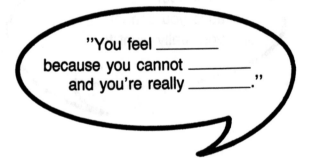

Personalizing Feelings

The personalizing process involves several internalizing steps: internalizing the personal implications for the child; internalizing the problem in terms of the child's response deficits; individualizing the goal in terms of response assets; individualizing the feeling in terms of the sadness or disappointment in experiencing response deficits and the eagerness or motivation to achieve the goal of response assets. Again, parenting is the process of transforming immature people to mature people. Maturity is a function of the person's response repertoire. So, therefore, parenting is the process of transforming a child's response deficits into assets. And personalizing is the heart of the process that affects this transformation.

Productive Parenting Emphasizes Personalizing Accurately

7. Parents as Initiators

One of parenting's high points can be the relief of watching matured adults face the world with courage and knowlege. The low point of parenting might be our sorrow as our frightened children seek escape from life's daily tasks. Another low point might be our anger at their rebellion as a result of our own lack of direction, or too much control. Parenting culminates in the products of our life efforts—our children. And they are a product of what they brought with them into this world, and how we taught them to use it—No more, No less! Parenting begins with life. It never ends.

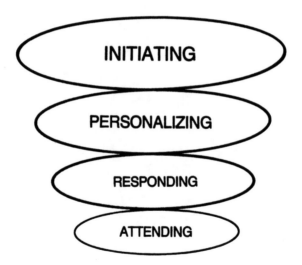

Parents are Initiators

Let us take a moment to get an index of how well we initiate in order to help our children achieve their personalized goals. Let us look at several personalized responses and see how we would go about initiating to achieve the personalized goals:

Personalized response: "You feel sad because you can't seem to be able to get her to be friendly and play with you, and you're really eager to be her friend."

Initiative response: _____
_____
_____
_____
_____

Personalized response: "You feel disappointed because you feel like you won't pass that test and the course and if you don't, you won't graduate this year. So you're real eager to learn how."

Initiative response: _____
_____
_____
_____
_____

Personalized response: "You feel happy because you're doing so well on the team now, and you're eager to do even better."

Initiative response: _____
_____
_____
_____

Developing Initiatives

You may have felt frustrated because you did not have the initiative responses you would like. And yet we must develop these responses in order to help our children achieve their goals.

You might have indicated to the child with a friendship problem:

> "Your goal is to make friends with her so that you can play with her everyday.
> Your first step is to greet her warmly each day.
> Your next steps are to find out what she likes to do so that you can do some of those things together."

You might have indicated to the child who cannot pass the test:

> "Your goal is to pass the test so that you can pass the course and graduate this year.
> Your first step is to find out what areas you are weak in.
> Your next steps are to set up a tutorial study and test-taking program to catch up on those areas."

You might have said to the child who is doing so well on the team:

> "Your goal is to do even better on the team.
> Your first step is to get a diagnosis from the coach of your strengths and weaknesses.
> Your next steps are to practice your weak areas and to put them together with your strong areas in better performances."

Developing Initiative With Our Children

You may have felt disappointed in yourself because you did not have the initiative responses you needed. But if you are eager to learn them, they are easily learned. The goal is to learn to make initiative responses with your children. The first step is to learn how to define the goal. The second step is to develop your initial steps. The third step is to develop the intermediary steps that will enable you to achieve your goal. And the final step is to take your steps. By learning the initiative steps, you will initiate with your children to facilitate their acting in order to achieve their goals.

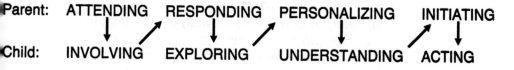

PARENTING SKILLS

Parent:	ATTENDING	RESPONDING	PERSONALIZING	INITIATING
Child:	INVOLVING	EXPLORING	UNDERSTANDING	ACTING

Initiating to Achieve Goals

The first step in initiating is defining the goal. Defining the goal allows us to measure our progress toward achieving the goal. We define the goal in terms that make it observable and measurable for the child. The basic ingredients follow:

Who is involved?
What are they doing?
Why and *how* are they doing it?
Where and *when* are they doing it?
How well are they doing it?

So for example, the child with the friendship problem (*who*) wants to make friends (*what*) so that they can play together (*why*) by relating interpersonally (*how*) every day (*where* and *when*) at accurate levels of empathy (*how well*). The child with the test-passing problem (*who*) wants to pass the test (*what*) so that he can pass the course (*why*) by learning to take tests (*how*) in school (*where* and *when*) and graduate this year (*how well*). After having defined the goal, it is simply a matter of using the communication format, "Your goal is _____," to communicate to your child.

GOAL

Who?
What?
Why and How?
Where and When?
How well?

"Your goal is _____."

Initiating Involves Defining Goals

The second step in initiating is developing the first step to achieve the goal. The first step must be a simple step. Otherwise, your child may fail at it and, thus, fail to achieve the goal. Indeed, the first step must be so simple as to seem very easy. Thus, for the child with the friendship problem, the first step is to greet the other person warmly. The first step for the child with the test-passing problem is to approach the teacher in order to find out his or her areas of weakness.

"Your first step is the *simplest step*."

GOAL

Who?
What?
Why and How?
Where and When?
How well?

Simplest Step

Initiating Involves Developing Initial Steps

The third step in initiating is developing the intermediary steps to achieve the goal. The intermediary steps are simply the large steps that the child must take to achieve the goal. Thus, for the child with the friendship problem, the intermediary steps include finding out what the other person likes and trying to do some of those things together. For the child with the test-passing problem, the intermediary steps include setting up tutorial, study and test-taking programs.

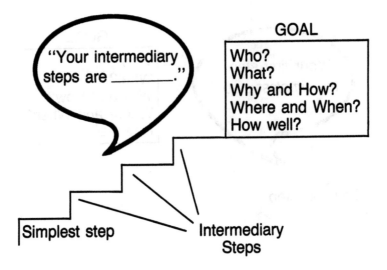

Initiating Involves Developing Intermediary Steps

The final step is actually taking the steps in the program to achieve the goal. As the child takes each step, he or she will see the intermediary steps more clearly. Then, the child can treat each intermediary step as a sub-goal and develop more detailed programs to achieve the sub-goal. As the child approaches each step, it is a good thing to remember the 3 R's of taking steps:

Review the steps to be taken to be sure that you include all of them.

Rehearse the steps to be taken to be sure that you are doing them correctly.

Repeat the steps after you have taken them to insure that you have mastered them.

Initiating Involves Taking Steps

The initiating program involves several operational steps: defining the goal in achievable terms; developing the initial simple step; developing an outline of the intermediary steps; and taking the steps and developing detailed steps to achieve each step. Again, parenting is the process of transforming children into mature people. We use our initiative skills to affect this transformation by helping our children act to achieve response assets.

Productive Parenting Emphasizes
Initiating Programmatically

IV. THE CONTENT OF PARENTING

8. Parents as Helpers

Parenting skills prepare parents for helping. Equipped with these skills, parents can help their children with problems in life. They help the children by using their interpersonal skills to facilitate the children's processing. They attend to their children's experiences in order to involve them in their problems. They respond to their children's experiences in order to facilitate their exploration of their experiences. They personalize their children's experiences in order to facilitate their understanding of their goals. They initiate with their children in order to help them act upon their programs.

LIVING

Helping With Problems in Living

Let us take some time to get an index of how we can facilitate our children's processing of problems in their lives. Let us describe briefly how we would go about supporting their activities. Think of a particular problem in life that your child has. Use the phases of processing to guide your thinking about facilitating living:

Facilitating involvement in living problems:

_____

_____

_____

Facilitating exploration of living problems:

_____

_____

_____

Facilitating understanding of living problems:

_____

_____

_____

Facilitating action upon living problems:

_____

_____

_____

Facilitating Processing

It is not easy to deal with the overwhelming problems of children today. The problems seem to intensify with each generation. Also, our relationships with our children can be complicated by their relationships with their peers. Perhaps most of all, the constantly changing environmental conditions, and the resulting and constant barrage of information, places burdens upon all of us—parent and child alike. What can we do in the face of these seemingly overwhelming odds? We can help our children live productively in their worlds. And we can do this by attempting to live productively in *our* worlds. We can do this by using our productive parenting skills.

Helping Children Live Productively

We use our parenting skills to facilitate the child's life skills development: attending to the child, in order to involve the child to be ready and prepared for living; responding to the child, in order to facilitate the child's exploration of his or her experience; personalizing the child's experience, in order to facilitate the child's understanding of his or her goals; and initiating, in order to facilitate the child's implementation of the programs to achieve the goals. We can facilitate the child's living experience by applying our parenting skills.

PHASES OF PARENTING

	Pre-Parenting	I	II	III
Parent:	ATTENDING	RESPONDING	PERSONALIZING	INITIATING
	↓	↓	↓	↓
Child:	INVOLVING in Readiness	EXPLORING Experience	UNDERSTANDING Goals	ACTING Upon Programs

Facilitating Our Children's Living

We can help our children prepare for living productively by considering the child's resources: physical, emotional, and intellectual. Physically, do our children have the proper rest, diet, and exercise to give them the highest levels of energy necessary for alertness? Emotionally, do our children have a level of motivation that enables them to be attentive to their life experiences? Intellectually, do our children have the life skills and resources necessary to live productively?

Physical
    Rest and Diet
    Exercise

Emotional
    Motivation
    Attentiveness

Intellectual
    Life Skills
    Resources

Involving Our Children in Living

For example, we may attend to our child in order to observe or listen for the answers to these questions. We may see the need for an improved diet, or more rest or exercise. We may observe motivational and attentiveness deficits. We may assess inadequacies of the child's life skills and resources to live productively. We may help design simple programs to facilitate readiness for living.

Physical
    Rest—8 hours
    Diet—Balanced
    Exercise—Regular

Emotional
    Motivation—Incentives
    Attentiveness—Discipline

Intellectual
    Life Skills—Skilling
    Resources—Provide

Facilitating Readiness

The most important thing we can do in helping our children explore their experiences is to help them to know where they are in relation to their worlds. We help them to do this by responding to their experiences. We respond to the content, expressed feelings and meaning of their experiences. We facilitate their exploration of personally relevant, concrete experiences. We facilitate their exploration with immediate response to their experiences. In other words, they immediately feel what they are talking about concretely.

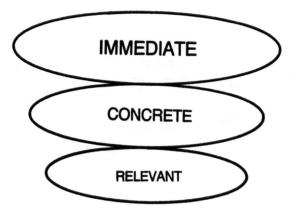

**Helping Our Children
Explore Experience**

If the young person has problems relating to his or her peers, the child may explore specific situations in which these problems occur. Further, the child may explore these experiences with the actual feelings the problems evoke. The child may say:

"No matter what I do, someone puts me down. No matter how good I try to be, it turns out bad. I just feel like giving up."

By responding accurately to these experiences, we facilitate the child's exploration of his or her experience.

"You feel pretty hopeless because the others are always putting you down."

Facilitating Exploration

In a similar manner, we can help our children understand their goals by personalizing their experiences. By personalizing their experiences, we help them understand where they are in relation to where they want or need to be with their experiences. We know that we have been successful in personalizing their experiences when they have internalized responsibility for the problem; expressed disappointment in their own past deficits; expressed an eagerness and readiness to assume responsibility to do something about their situations.

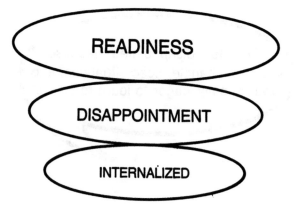

READINESS

DISAPPOINTMENT

INTERNALIZED

Helping Our Children Understand Goals

For example, the child with social problems may express significant concern over his or her situation:

"I just don't seem to be able to get through the day without one of them picking on me. They just seem to be tougher than I am."

By personalizing the child's experience, we facilitate the child's understanding of his or her problems and goals.

"I really want to get on with things, because I can't stand being the way I am any longer."

"You feel disappointed, because you can't handle these situations, and you're really eager to learn to do so."

Facilitating Understanding

Finally, we are most helpful when we can help our
children act upon programs to achieve their goals. By
initiating, we help them to get from where they are to
where they want or need to be. We initiate by helping
them define their goals and develop and implement
their programs. We also help by encouraging them to
process feedback as a consequence of their acting.

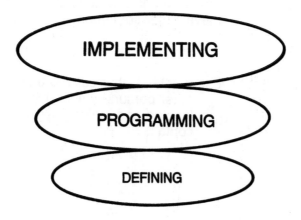

Helping Our Children Act Upon Programs

The child with social problems may be helped to develop and implement a program that will improve his or her life skills.

"Your goal is to be able to relate better so that you can have friends. You can do this by being attentive to them during and after school at levels that communicate interest.

Your steps are to attend, observe and listen.

Your first step is to attend physically to the other person by squaring, leaning and making eye contact."

Facilitating Action

Productive parenting, then, helps us to develop our children's life skills. We do this by using our parenting skills to facilitate their exploring, understanding and acting. In the process, we gain in our own life skills. Ultimately, we will teach our children everything that we have learned. That is the culmination of parenting. Hopefully, in their maturity, they will teach us everything that they have learned.

Productive Parenting Facilitates Life Skills

9. Parents as Teachers

Perhaps the single most important thing that parents can do to facilitate their children's actualization of resources is to encourage excellence in performance. The area does not matter; it may be athletics, the arts, or a specific intellectual pursuit. It may be only in one one area; excellence need not be encouraged in all areas initially. By pursuing one area to a level of excellence, the benefits of actualization of resources will become clear for the child. Physically, these ingredients involve a lot of hard work. Emotionally, they demand a high level of discipline. Intellectually, they require a high level of skills development. By achieving excellence in any one area, the child is then able to transfer in later life to all areas of endeavor. Thus, in maturity, the adult is able to develop his or her own resources.

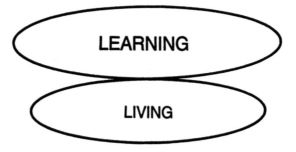

Helping Our Children With Learning Skills

Let us take some time to get an index of how we can
facilitate our children's learning. Let us describe in
some detail how we would go about supporting their
learning activities. Think of a particular learning experience in which your child is or might be involved.
Use the phases of learning to guide your thinking about
facilitating learning:

Facilitative involvement in learning _____

_____

_____

Facilitative exploration in learning _____

_____

_____

Facilitative understanding in learning _____

_____

_____

Facilitative action in learning _____

_____

_____

Facilitating Learning

You may have found it easier to facilitate the involvement phase than the exploration, understanding and action phases. After all, most of us are not professional teachers. Yet there are many things that you may have thought of to get your child ready and motivated to learn: exposure at home to books and intelligent conversation; direct emphasis on the importance of educational excellence; direct influence on the development of the work ethic and discipline values. These are all very important in motivating the child to want to learn. And the parent is the most significant source of this motivation for learning. But how, concretely, can we facilitate the actual process of the child's learning? That is the task at hand.

We use the same parenting skills to facilitate the child's learning: attending to the child, in order to prepare the child for learning; responding to the child, in order to facilitate the child's exploration of the learning experience; personalizing the child's experience, in order to facilitate the definition of the learning objectives; and initiating, in order to facilitate the child's implementation of a program to achieve mastery of learning. We can facilitate the child's learning, and support the schooling experience, by learning these parenting skills applications.

PHASES OF PARENTING

	Pre-Parenting	I	II	III
Parent:	ATTENDING	RESPONDING	PERSONALIZING	INITIATING
	↓	↓	↓	↓
Child:	INVOLVING	EXPLORING	UNDERSTANDING	ACTING
	for	Learning	Learning	Upon
	Learning	Experience	Objectives	Learning
	Readiness			Programs

Facilitating Our Children's Learning

Perhaps the greatest contribution toward preparing our children for learning is to help them become aware of the basic rules of skills and knowledge. Skills are observable and measurable actions which the learners perform. Here, knowledge is comprised of the facts, concepts and principles which support the skill performance.

CATEGORIES	LEVELS	DEFINITION
SKILLS	Skill Steps	—Steps which the learners must take to perform the skill
	Skill Objectives	—Operations that define the skills to be performed
KNOWLEDGE	Principles	—Processes that relate antecedents and consequences among and between facts and concepts
	Concepts	—The meanings or relationships—usually adjectives, verbs or adverbs—which we attach to things that tell us about the things and what they do
	Facts	—Name or labels—usually nouns—which identify what a thing is

Helping Our Children
Get Ready for Learning

In interpersonal skills, the aspects of responding comprise the skill. In turn, responding to content, feeling and meaning comprises the skill steps. The principle of reciprocal responsiveness supports the skill performance:

If we respond to the experience of others, then they will attempt to respond to our experience so that we may relate more productively.

The supportive concepts include responding to content, feeling and meaning. The supportive facts emphasize the identification of the people involved.

CATEGORIES	LEVELS	ILLUSTRATION
SKILLS	Skill Steps	—Responding to content, feeling and meaning
	Skill Objectives	—Responding skill operations
KNOWLEDGE	Principles	—Reciprocal responsiveness
	Concepts	—Responding to content, feeling, meaning
	Facts	—People who are relating

Facilitating Awareness

With this comprehension of skills and knowledge, there are three essential steps that we can take to respond in order to help our children explore or diagnose where they are in the learning process. The first involves the skill performance itself: can the child perform the skill? The second involves the child's explanation of his or her performance: can the child describe all of the skill steps and all of the supportive knowledge needed to perform the skill steps? The third involves the question of additional instruction: does the child know all that he or she needs to know to perform the skill? If the answer to all of these questions is "Yes!", then the child has mastered this learning and is ready to move on to the next learning. If the answer to any of these questions is "No," then the child requires additional instruction.

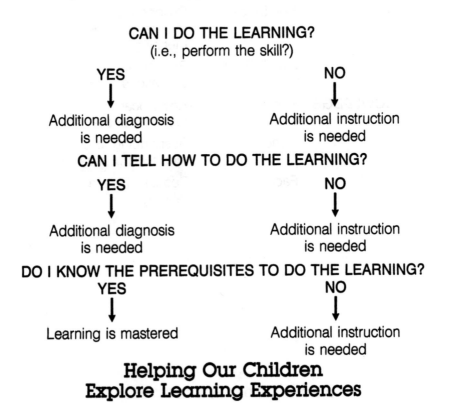

CAN I DO THE LEARNING?
(i.e., perform the skill?)

YES — Additional diagnosis is needed

NO — Additional instruction is needed

CAN I TELL HOW TO DO THE LEARNING?

YES — Additional diagnosis is needed

NO — Additional instruction is needed

DO I KNOW THE PREREQUISITES TO DO THE LEARNING?

YES — Learning is mastered

NO — Additional instruction is needed

**Helping Our Children
Explore Learning Experiences**

We may diagnose the learners' assets and deficits in responding skills. We may diagnose by assessing the learners' ability to *do, tell* and *know* the skill. Depending upon the results, the individual learners will receive further diagnosis and/or instruction.

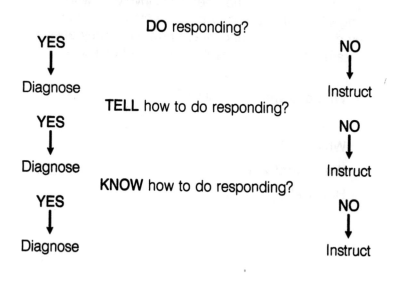

Diagnosing Learning Deficits

Personalizing our children's experiences helps them to understand their learning objectives. Personalizing emphasizes defining the method of putting the skill into operation. We define the skill objective to be learned in the same manner that we define any objective. We use systematic terms for the operations involved: *who* is doing what; *what* are they doing; *why* and *how* are they doing it; *where* and *when*; *how well*. They answer the same basic questions that we asked earlier.

Who and **what** is involved?

What are they doing?

Why and **how** are they doing it?

Where and **when**

How well?

Helping Our Children Understand Learning Objectives

For example, the interpersonal skills learning objective may be outlined in terms of the operational dimensions as follows:

Who?	— The learners
What?	— will learn to respond to others' experience
Why?	— in order to relate productively to others
How?	— by responding to content, feeling and meaning
Where?	— at home and in school
When?	— during hours
How well?	— at levels interchangeable with the other person's experience.

Defining Learning Objectives

There are six steps that we can take to ensure that our children acquire the skills of learning. First, get an overview or a preview of the skills to be learned. Second, get someone to tell how to perform the skill. Third, get someone to show how to perform the skill. Fourth, get an opportunity to do or perform the skill. Fifth, get feedback from the teachers or experts. Sixth, practice the skill until mastered. Clearly, there are other steps needed to accomplish the ultimate purposes of the learning objective, one of which is to apply the skill in a real-life setting, and perhaps to transfer the skill to other contexts. However, these six steps will ensure that the child has acted to acquire the skills involved in the learning objective.

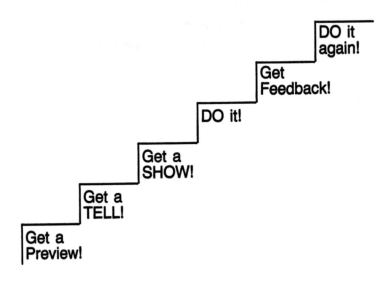

DO it again!

Get Feedback!

DO it!

Get a SHOW!

Get a TELL!

Get a Preview!

**Helping Our Children
Acquire Learning Skills**

For example, in attempting to acquire responding skills, the learners may employ the acquisition program seen below. As can be seen, the *Hear—See—Do* steps constitute the heart of the acquisition program. *Hearing* creates an awareness. *Seeing* provides a model. *Doing* accomplishes skills acquisition. Ultimately, we apply the skills to the skills objective.

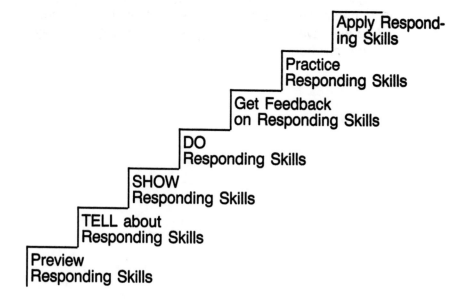

Acquiring Learning Skills

Productive parenting, then, emphasizes facilitating learning. This includes involving the child for readiness; exploring the learning experience; understanding the learning objectives; and acting to acquire the skill and knowledge. When we are able to facilitate our children in developing these learning skills, then we can assist the formal learning processes that take place in school and elsewhere. When the children learn to acquire, apply and transfer these learning skills, then they have the necessary skills to guide their further development. And we have facilitated the goal of parenting—maturity in our children!

Productive Parenting Emphasizes Facilitating Learning

10. Parents as Workers

Excellence in learning translates directly to productivity in career and working achievement. The mature adult is a productive adult. The mature adult produces more than he or she consumes. Indeed, the mature adult is concerned with overconsumption: in the family, community, region, nation and the world. The mature adult is concerned with minimizing the input of resources, both human and natural, and maximizing the output of benefits, both human and natural. The mature adult is concerned with the freedom of choice for the process between the input and the output.

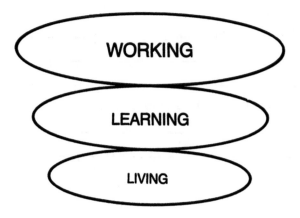

Let us take some time to get an index of how we can support our children's careers. Let us describe in some detail how we would go about supporting their career or working conditions. Assume a particular work experience in which your children might be involved. Use the phases of learning to guide our thinking about supporting their careers:

Facilitating involvement in careers _____

_____

_____

Facilitating exploration in careers _____

_____

_____

Facilitating understanding in careers _____

_____

_____

Facilitating action in careers _____

_____

_____

Again, you may have found it easier to support involvement than the exploration, understanding and action phases. You might feel overwhelmed by these latter phases, because it is hard to imagine how you can help your children in career-related activities. You might be able to see how you can model a healthy attitude about career development. You might also hold discussions with your children to explore career activities. But it may be very difficult to conceive of how you can help them understand and plan to achieve their career goals. How can we concretely support our children's career development processes?

Helping Our Children Develop Careers

We use the same parenting skills to support the child's career development: attending to the child in order to involve the child in preparing for a career; responding to the child in order to facilitate the child's exploration of career opportunities; personalizing the child's experience to help him or her select preferred objectives; and initiating in order to facilitate the child's planning for a productive career. We can support the child's career experience by learning these applications of parenting skills.

PHASES OF PARENTING

	Pre-Parenting	I	II	III
Parenting Skills:	ATTENDING ↓	RESPONDING ↓	PERSONALIZING ↓	INITIATING ↓
Working Skills:	INVOLVING for Career Readiness	EXPLORING Career Experience	UNDERSTANDING Career Objectives	ACTING Career Programs

Supporting Our Children's Career Efforts

We can support our children's entry into the career development process by using our attending skills to help them become aware of career alternatives. Awareness of career alternatives means expanding both the *areas* and *levels* of career alternatives. The areas of career alternatives include any area which the child might consider for a career. Generally, the child will begin by considering the areas he or she has been exposed to, at home or in school or in the community. The point is to expand the areas of consideration so that the child has a better chance of satisfying his or her values and talents. Career alternatives include all the different levels at which a child might enter an area, depending upon his or her education. For example, a person may strive for many levels of alternatives within one occupational area, e.g., technology. By expanding in this manner, the child can find the level within an area to which he or she aspires. (See Table on page 136.)

**Helping Our Children
Get Ready for Careers**

CAREER ALTERNATIVES

AREAS OF INTEREST

LEVELS OF EDUCATION	Service (Contact)	Education	Business Recreation	Business	Technology	Outdoor (Detail)	Science
Graduate School							
4-Yr. College							
Jr. College							
Vocational Technical							
High School							
Less than H.S.							

For example, the young person may wish to examine levels of alternatives within just one occupational area, technology. We can view a sample of thousands of alternatives within the one area. The computer technology area yields different definitions of tasks and responsibilities at different levels of education. By becoming aware of the different levels of careers within different areas of interest, the youth can find the level of an area to which he or she aspires.

LEVELS OF EDUCATION	AREA OF INTEREST
	Technology (Computer)
Grad. School	Systems Designer
4-Year College	Systems Analyst
Jr. College	Computer Programmer
Voc. Tech.	Computer Operator
High School	Key Punch Operator
Less than High School	Maintenance Worker

Facilitating Awareness

By using our responding skills to facilitate exploration of their career experience, we can help our youth become aware of where they are in relation to working experiences. By selecting the level of education to which the youth aspires, they can begin to explore career options within that level.

LEVELS OF EDUCATION	TECHNOLOGY AREA
Grad School or 4-Year College	Systems Analyst Medical Technologist Engineer
Jr. College	Computer Programmer X-Ray Technician Dental Technician
Voc. Tech.	Computer Operator Instrument Repair Machinist
High School	Key Punch Operator Carpet Layer Factory Inspector
Less than High School	Assembly Line Worker Service Station Attendant Maintenance Worker

Helping Our Children Explore Career Alternatives

The youth may begin to explore occupations at the junior or community college levels of the technology area.

LEVEL OF EDUCATION	AREA OF INTEREST
	Technology
Jr. College	Computer Programmer
	X-Ray Technician
	Dental Technician

Within that level, the youth may explore career alternatives by seeking out sources of expertise—people who work in the area, recommended books, or data files. The youth may ask the operational questions concerning the tasks to be performed. These questions may be framed in the terms employed in the private sector.

What are the **components?** — **Who** and **what** is involved?

What are the **functions?** — **What** are they doing?

What are the **processes?** — **Why** and **how** are they doing it?

What are the **conditions?** — **Where** and **when?**

What are the **standards?** — **How well?**

Facilitating Exploration

By using our personalizing skills to facilitate their understanding of their career goals, we can help our youth to decide upon a preferred career alternative. That way they will understand where they want or need to be. They can select a career alternative by deciding upon their major occupational values and determining how the alternatives impact those values. It may be helpful to think of the values in physical, emotional and intellectual terms.

CAREER ALTERNATIVES

VALUES	I	II	III
Physical			
Emotional			
Intellectual			

**Helping Our Children
Understand Career Goals**

Our children may choose among the three career alternatives by developing some critical values about salary, teamwork, or the opportunity for creativity. As can be seen from an evaluation of courses in terms of positive (+), negative (-) and neutral impact (0), the position of computer programmer impacts most favorably upon the youth's values. Developing a career in computer programming could become a career goal for this particular youth.

CAREER ALTERNATIVES

Values	I Computer Programmer	II X-Ray Technician	III Dental Technician
Salary	+ +	+	+
Teamwork	+	+	+
Creativity	+ +	+	0

Facilitating Understanding

The youth may prepare for becoming a computer programer by planning a work study program: seeking sources of expertise, studying in college, specializing in computer laboratory work, and, finally, working part-time in computer programming. The youth is now acting upon his or her career program.

CAREER OBJECTIVE

Who?	Programmer
What?	develops software
Why & How?	by computer science
Where & When?	with work constraints
How well?	to meet end-user specs

Work part-time in
computer programming

Specialize in
computer lab work

Study in
Jr. College

Seek sources
of expertise

Facilitating Action

Finally, by using our initiating skills to facilitate their acting upon their career programs, we can help our youth to plan and prepare for their chosen careers. That way they will know how to get from where they are to where they want or need to be. Again, they can define their career objective in terms of the operational dimensions. They can then develop the career programs to achieve the career objective.

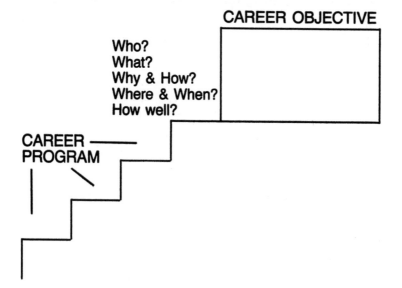

CAREER OBJECTIVE

Who?
What?
Why & How?
Where & When?
How well?

CAREER ———
PROGRAM

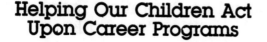

**Helping Our Children Act
Upon Career Programs**

Productive parenting, then, emphasizes supporting working. This includes involving the child in the process of exploring the career alternatives, understanding the career goal, and acting to become productive in the selected career. When the children learn to acquire, apply and transfer working skills, then they have the working skills to guide their own career maturational process. And we have succeeded in our parenting goals of transforming our children into mature adults!

Productive Parenting Emphasizes Working Skills

V. THE DEVELOPMENTAL PROCESS

11. Helping the Community Grow

One sign of maturity in parents is their support of community growth. The parents do this not just for themselves, although they benefit from that growth. They do this not just for their children, although their concern for their children may lead them to community concerns. They do this because they begin to see their community as a family. And, as parents, they become concerned with what is happening to their community, and the children in it. As mature adults, they become involved and expand the boundaries of their own families. They intervene because they are committed to helping other people mature. And they can successfully act upon this commitment, because they have parenting skills.

Parenting is Helping the Community Grow

Let us reflect upon how we would relate to the community in order to help it grow more effectively. We can use our parenting skills to guide us through a developmental process of involving, exploring, understanding and acting:

Attending to get involved in the community _____

_____

_____

Responding to explore where the community is _____

_____

_____

Personalizing to understand where the community wants or needs to be _____

_____

_____

Initiating to act to achieve community goals _____

_____

_____

Perhaps you find it difficult to get involved in these community issues in any systematic way. Maybe you don't know enough about organizing a community to grow effectively. Perhaps you could join parent-teacher associations and attend school committee meetings. Maybe you've even thought of becoming involved in the town council or in some of the community relations activities of the local businesses. But it may not seem enough to make a difference.

Relating to the Community

Perhaps it still seems impossible that just a few people could change a community. You may feel overwhelmed because you do not have all of the resources to affect such changes. Clearly, before you need to call upon these resources in action programs, you need to understand your goals for community change. Before you can understand your goals, you must have explored your community needs, and before you have explored your community needs, you must have attended to your community. The same parenting skills that will help your children grow will help your community grow.

PHASES OF PARENTING

	Pre-Parenting	I	II	III
Parenting Skills:	ATTENDING ↓	RESPONDING ↓	PERSONALIZING ↓	INITIATING ↓
Citizen:	INVOLVING in the Community	EXPLORING Community Needs	UNDERSTANDING Community Goals	ACTING to Achieve Community Goals

Helping the Community Grow

Parents and children are subject to many turbulent influences. Before we can do anything else, we must attend to the community in order to get involved with its various components. There are many components—some very significant sources of effect—in special instances. But most of the community effectiveness is accounted for by four sources: the children (as recipients of whatever provisions are being made), the parents, school, and business/government, which are as various "delivery" mechanisms at different points in time. Once we have the components, it is a matter of ordering their functions.

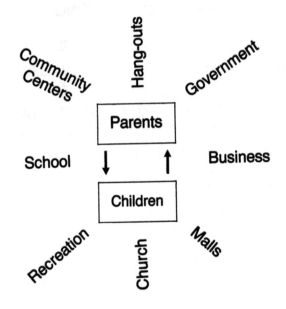

Attending to the Community

When we explore the community's needs, we find we can now impose some order. It is clear to us that we as parents are the primary providers of living skills to our children:

Parents

↓

Children

It is also clear that the school is the primary source of providing learning skills to our children as learners.

School

↓

Learners

Finally, it is clear that business/industry and government are the primary sources of working skills to our children as adults:

Business & Government

↓

Adults

Responding in Order to Explore Community Needs

As we look at each of these delivery systems, our needs are transformed into goals, both within and between the various components. Within the components, we find that the people do not always have the skills to accept their responsibilities. Between the components, we find that they do not support each other when one is making a delivery. Thus, an ideal situation for community growth and development would be one in which each component had the skills to make or support the appropriate deliveries.

At the level of living skills development, parents require parenting skills; school, business and government need living support skills, and the children need living skills.

DEVELOPMENTAL LEVEL

COMPONENTS

Living Skills

| School | → | Parents | ← | Bus. & Gov't. |

↓

| Children |

Personalizing to Understand Living Skills Goals

At the level of learning skills development, teachers need teaching skills and the administrators need management and supervisory skills. Parents and business and government need the learning support skills. Students need learning skills.

**DEVELOPMENTAL
LEVEL**

COMPONENTS

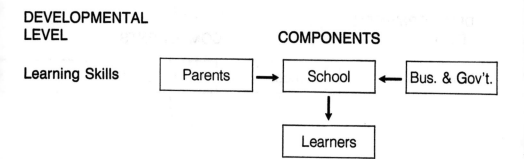

Learning Skills

Parents → School ← Bus. & Gov't.

Learners

Personalizing to Understand Learning Skills Goals

At the level of working skills development, business and government employees need management and supervisory skills. Parents and schools need working support skills, and the adult workers need working skills.

**DEVELOPMENTAL
LEVEL**   **COMPONENTS**

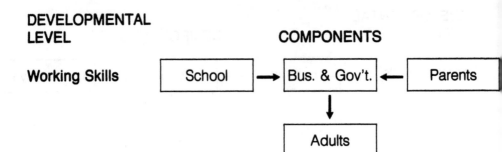

Working Skills

| School | → | Bus. & Gov't. | ← | Parents |

| Adults |

Personalizing to Understand
Working Skills Goals

When we have the goal of developing delivery and support skills programs at all living, learning and working levels, we can proceed to develop programs to achieve these objectives. We must develop specific programs to meet the unique needs within each component of every delivery and support system. These programs must be designed inclusively to incorporate input and feedback from all people involved in the intended outcome. For example, in schools, the teachers, administrators, and counselors, as well as the parents, and business and government, must have input into the teaching skills program. It is similar with all other components, as we transform our visions of community growth into inclusive models that can be implemented effectively in the everyday world. That way we can make the everyday world something special.

Initiating to Act to Achieve Community Goals

Productive parenting, then, emphasizes community development. Community development includes attending in order to become involved, responding to explore community needs, personalizing to understand community goals, and initiating the achievement of community goals. When we use our parenting skills to influence the development of the community, we are not only effecting ourselves and our children; we are extending the boundaries of our family and, indeed, our humanity to include everyone within our reach who effects the children. Thus, we become parents to the maturational process of our own community.

Productive Parenting Emphasizes Community Development

12. Teaching Parenting Skills

The sign of our children's maturity is when they indicate a readiness to "parent" themselves. A sign of the parent's maturity is the teaching of parenting·skills: training themselves out of their jobs by teaching their children the skills to become mature adults.

There is a time to change and grow. And that time comes when our children mature to young adulthood. Then, we teach them the parenting skills that we supported them with throughout their lives. Then, we must grow to our next developmental level by applying the skills we already have, and by developing new skills.

Parenting is Teaching Parenting Skills

Let us reflect upon how we would deliver parenting skills to our children. We can use our parenting skills while we are teaching them:

Helping our children to attend to get involved _____

_____

_____

Helping our children to respond to explorations of where people are _____

_____

_____

Helping our children to personalize their understanding of where people want or need to be _____

_____

_____

Helping our children to initiate to act to achieve people's goals _____

_____

_____

Relating to the Child's
Need to be an Adult

Y̶ou may find it easier to apply your parenting skills
when you are helping your children to acquire them.
While you offer them your parenting skills, you also
teach them those skills. That way, they take advantage
of all sources of learning: the experiential, in the sense
that they have experienced it; the modeling, in the
respect that they can model themselves after you; and
the didactic, in the respect that you teach and shape
the skills directory.

Developing Parenting Skills Programs

Using our parenting skills to *teach* parenting skills means: we are not going to simply impose our parenting skills upon our children, we are going to customize our parenting skills to meet their unique needs. This means that we are going to use our parenting skills to facilitate our children's movement through exploration, understanding and action. Then we are going to tailor our teaching of parenting skills to meet their unique parenting goals. In other words, we are actually going to function as effective teachers: first, relating to the learners' frames of reference; then relating our content instrumentally to their purposes. When we become teachers, we are going to help our children to become parents.

PHASES OF PARENTING

Skills	Pre-Parenting	I	II	III
Parent:	ATTENDING ↓	RESPONDING ↓	PERSONALIZING ↓	INITIATING ↓
Child:	INVOLVING the Children's Experiences	EXPLORING Children's Parenting Needs	UNDERSTANDING to Develop Children's Parenting Goals	ACTING to Teach Children Parenting Skills

Teaching Parenting Skills

We will begin by teaching our children precisely the parenting skills we learned ourselves: to attend to other people in order to involve them in a learning process. You will recall that we attend to people through physical attentiveness or positioning, through observing their appearance and behavior and making references from their levels of attending, and by listening to their expression of their experience. We will teach our children all of these attending skills in a manner tailored to their unique parenting goals.

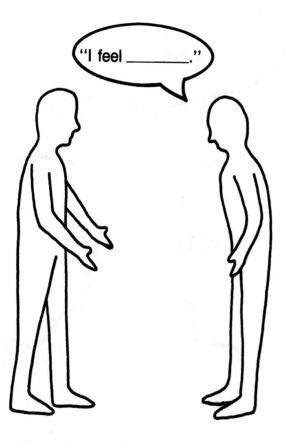

Attending to Involve People

We will continue by teaching our children responding skills. We will recall that responding skills include responding to content, responding to feeling, and responding to feeling and meaning. We will teach our children all of the responding skills in a manner tailored to their unique parenting goals.

Responding in Order to Help
People Explore Where They Are

We will continue further by teaching our children personalizing skills. You will recall that personalizing skills
include personalizing the meaning or the implications
for people, personalizing the problem or the response
deficit, personalizing the goal or the response asset,
personalizing the new feeling. We will teach our children all of the personalizing skills tailored to their
unique parenting goals.

"You feel disappointed because you cannot handle this situation and you really want to."

Personalizing to Help People Understand Their Goals

You will conclude by teaching initiative skills. Initiative skills include defining the goal, developing the first step, developing the intermediary steps, and taking the steps. We will teach our children all of the initiative skills tailored to their unique parenting goals.

Initiating to Help People
Act to Achieve Their Goals

Productive parenting, then, emphasizes teaching parenting skills. The parenting skills to be taught include attending to people, in order to involve them in a learning experience; responding to people, in order to help people explore where they are; personalizing understanding, in order to help them understand where they want or need to be, and initiating action programs,to help them get to where they want or need to be. When we teach our children parenting skills, we bring the parenting cycle around full circle: we teach our children to be parents for themselves and others. We prepare them not only to live in a world much different from the one in which we lived; but also, by equipping them with all of the responses they need to create a much different world and, hopefully, much better than the one in which we lived!

Productive Parenting Emphasizes Teaching Parenting Skills

VI. SUMMARY & CONCLUSIONS

13. Productive Parenting

Perhaps a most difficult realization for many people is that their parents are growing old. Physically, they may not be as fit and robust as they once were. Indeed, we may be surprised as our parents shrink in size before our very eyes. Emotionally, we worry that they may become less stable and more egocentric. Intellectually, we are afraid that they may become more rigid and ir-rational than they once were. To be sure, depending upon our parenting skills, they may ultimately take on some of the characteristics that we once had as chil-dren when they were parenting us. The prospective role-reversal in parenting can be a troublesome burden.

Parent-Rearing is Growing

The real crisis is ours. Can we grow to fully accept the implications of parenting? Can we become our own parents and, in so doing, shepherd our parents through their most difficult moments? Again, these crises, like all other crisis in parenting, are only opportunities to grow—for us and for our parents! So when we deal with their declining sensitivities for others, increasingly sensitized concern for themselves, declining industriousness or inappropriate initiatives, or the many other characteristics that may present problems, we must remember that these crises are opportunities for us to reach toward our next level of development. Somehow we must rise above our conditioned responses and help our parents rise above their reflex responses. As in child-rearing, how well we grow together or how far we fall apart depends upon our parenting skills.

Crises are Opportunities to Grow

Think for a moment of the traditional roles of young parents and elderly parents. Write down the three key words that define each of their potential contributions for you. Then circle your key word and write a definition using the word. If your spouse or other people are involved, try to write a definition that includes all of the key words.

Young Parent: Key Words:

_____

_____

_____

Definition: A young parent is _____

_____

_____

_____

Elderly Parent: Key Words:

_____

_____

_____

Definition: An elderly parent is _____

_____

_____

_____

Young and Old Parents Make Contributions

You may have found that you used familiar words in each of these definitions. The young parent may be seen as fully involved in life and thus, physically active and engaged; emotionally open and involved; intellectually focused and programmatic. In turn, the elderly parent may be seen as a veteran of life and, thus, having experienced more physically; having expanded his or her humanity, emotionally; having developed a wisdom in perspective, intellectually. In short, the young parent is the doer and must, because of his or her many tasks, be somewhat exclusive in focus. The elderly parent, having accomplished the larger part of his or her workload, may be more inclusive in his or her deliberations. While the young have the capability of acting, the elderly offer potentially broad and inclusive dimensions of exploration and understanding.

Young and Old Parents Have Traditional Roles

The function of parent-rearing is the same as child-rearing: to transform immature people into mature people. Again, immaturity simply means that people lack the responses to function effectively in their worlds. In order to help them to function effectively in their worlds, we must use our parenting skills. We must employ the same responding, personalizing and initiating skills that we employed in child-rearing. When we do so, the mysteries of life will be revealed to us—in part by doing—and in part through the wisdom that our parents will share with us.

Parent-Rearing is Growing People

When we respond to our parents, we transform their fears of loneliness and isolation into finely-tuned sensitivities to their own as well as our families' needs and aspirations. When we help our parents to personalize their problems, we find that they have their own unique and individualized goals at different developmental levels of dependence or independence. When we help our parents initiate to achieve their goals, we find that they are resourceful and motivated. When we treat our parents as skilled human beings, we find that they live, learn and work in very intense ways. When we use our parenting skills to treat our parents as maturing human beings, we find that they continue to make successive approximations of actualizing their physical, emotional and intellectual resources. We treat them as we would have had them treat us.

Parenting is Helping People Actualize Their Resources

When we use our parenting skills to facilitate our
parents' actualization of their resources, we are asking
them for their contributions in helping us understand
the world in which we live. As adults we have managed
only to isolate ourselves in a corner of this fragile
spacecraft called Earth: anticipating the expiration of its
finite natural resources while more than two-thirds of its
poverty-stricken population anticipate each and every
night the death by starvation of any or all of their family
members. We are all waiting for the nuclear destruction
that threatens each and every man, woman and child
on Earth. Those of us who undertake stress of daily living need the perspective of those who have been
through it, and now have the opportunity to reflect
upon it—the elderly.

Parenting Yields Parental Understanding

Similarly, when we use our parenting skills to teach our children all that we know about our world, we are asking them to create a world which we will not know. Our only hope to live fully in the days allocated to us—the only hope for the survival, let alone growth of future generations—is for us to teach our children all of our positive responses. Then we can hope that they will put these responses together in combinations that we could not even anticipate, and in doing so create a new and truly human world, one that is responsive to human experience, personalizing of human goals, and the initiative of human achievement.

Parenting Yields Children's Hopes

We see that productive parenting skills are much more than child-rearing skills. They are the prototype for human existence. They are the essence of our humanity, the ingredients of life itself. Productive parenting skills are the skills that enable us to expand the boundaries of our humanity to include all human life, indeed, all of nature. Productive parenting skills are the skills that enable us to do that one thing that distinguishes the human condition: choose. The choice is whether we will use our resources to live and actualize our humanity in our own time. Or to die, impotent, hopeless, trapped in our own selves. We make the choice daily in the way we treat our children, our parents, ourselves.

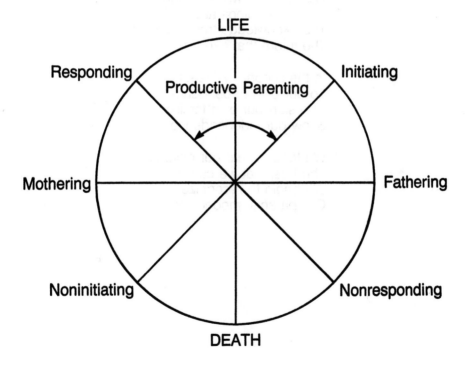

Parenting is a Matter of Life and Death

Thank You, Parents

There are at least three phases
To every person's life,
The first and third with parents
The second with a spouse.

In the first we are guided
By parent's nourishment,
Achievements of our parents,
Until we're flourishing.

We sit down with our parents
And learn things at their knees,
Their knowledge from the past,
The future that can be.

In the second we react
To our own dependence,
And start our own families,
Show our independence.

We tend to rear our children
The best that we can do.
We begin to recognize
Our parents' model true.

We turn again to parents,
The third and final phase.
Hear again the wisdom
They learned along their ways.

We sit again with parents
And learn things at their knees,
Their knowledge from the past,
The future that can be.

Life becomes a circle
A cycle to rephase,
Repeat again the learning
Until our final days.

For what is life if not
An opportunity to say,
"Thank you, parents
For helping develop me."

But our real thanks will come
In how we use our days,
How we rear our families,
The third and final phase.

R.R.C.